Journal British Cine Television

Volume 11.4 · 2014

Channel 4 and British Film Culture

Issue Editors

Paul McDonald
and
Justin Smith

Edinburgh University Press

Subscription rates for 2015

Four issues per year, published in January, April, July and October

		Tier	UK	EUR	RoW	N. America
Institutions	Print & online	1	£137.50	£150.30	£158.90	$270.00
		2	£171.50	£184.30	£192.90	$328.00
		3	£214.00	£226.80	£235.40	$400.00
		4	£257.00	£269.80	£278.40	$473.50
		5	£291.00	£303.80	£312.40	$531.00
	Online	1	£116.50	£116.50	£116.50	$198.00
		2	£145.50	£145.50	£145.50	$247.50
		3	£182.00	£182.00	£182.00	$309.50
		4	£218.50	£218.50	£218.50	$371.50
		5	£247.50	£247.50	£247.50	$421.00
	Additional print volumes		£120.00	£132.85	£141.45	$240.50
	Single issues		£47.50	£51.00	£53.00	$90.00
Individuals	Print		£61.50	£74.50	£83.00	$141.00
	Online		£61.50	£61.50	£61.50	$104.50
	Print & online		£76.50	£89.50	£98.00	$166.50
	Back issues/ single copies		£17.00	£20.00	£22.50	$38.50

How to order

Subscriptions can be accepted for complete volumes only. Print prices include packing and airmail for subscribers outside the UK. Volumes back to the year 2000 (where applicable) are included in online prices. Print back volumes will be charged at the current volume subscription rate.

All orders must be accompanied by the correct payment. You can pay by cheque in Pound Sterling or US Dollars, bank transfer, Direct Debit or Credit/Debit Card. The individual rate applies only when a subscription is paid for with a personal cheque, credit card or bank transfer.

To order using the online subscription form, please visit www.euppublishing.com/page/jbctv/subscribe. Alternatively you may place your order by telephone on +44 (0)131 650 4196, fax on +44 (0)131 662 3286 or email to journals@eup.ed.ac.uk using your Visa or Mastercard credit card. Don't forget to include the expiry date of your card, the security number (three digits on the reverse of the card) and the address that the card is registered to.

Please make your cheque payable to Edinburgh University Press Ltd. Sterling cheques must be drawn on a UK bank account.

If you would like to pay by bank transfer or Direct Debit, contact us at journals@eup.ed.ac.uk and we will provide instructions.

Advertising

Advertisements are welcomed and rates are available on request, or by consulting our website at www.euppublishing.com. Advertisers should send their enquiries to the Journals Marketing Manager at the address above.

Contents

This publication is available as a book (ISBN 978-0-7486-9251-4) or as a single issue or part of a subscription to *Journal of British Cinema and Television*, Volume 11 (ISSN: 1743-4521). Please visit www.euppublishing.com/journal/jbctv for more information.

Introduction

Justin Smith and Paul McDonald

When Channel 4, the UK's fourth national television network, was launched in 1982 its policy of commissioning new feature films for television broadcast and selective cinema release marked a shift in British film culture. Widely credited with revitalising a moribund UK film industry, the initiative represented a new intervention on the part of a public service broadcaster and, in turn, redefined the place of film on television with landmark programming strands from *Film on Four* to the *Eleventh Hour*. Channel 4 withstood early criticism from some industry voices such as director Alan Parker, producer Don Boyd and the then Managing Director the National Film Finance Corporation Mamoun Hassan (Houston et al. 1984: 115–22); the tenor of their complaints was that television film would diminish the cinematic experience. Negative publicity was also aroused by Channel 4's decision to schedule acquired feature films which some judged to be unsuitable for television broadcast. Yet by 1987 the Channel's contribution to European cinema was recognised with the conferring of the Roberto Rossellini award at the Cannes film festival. Since then the international box office and award successes of many Film4 titles (from *My Beautiful Laundrette* (1985), *The Crying Game* (1992) and *Four Weddings and Funeral* (1993), to *Trainspotting* (1995), *Slumdog Millionaire* (2008) and *12 Years a Slave* (2013)) have made Film4 synonymous with a rejuvenated national cinema and established television subsidy

Journal of British Cinema and Television 11.4 (2014): 413–417
Edinburgh University Press
DOI: 10.3366/jbctv.2014.0226
© *Journal of British Cinema and Television*
www.euppublishing.com/jbctv

(alongside BBC Films) as a vital cornerstone of government film policy (DCMS 2012).

Inside Channel 4, the Film4 brand has proved durable, adapting to the more commercial orientation taken by the broadcaster from the early 1990s, and surviving the misfortunes of an experimental phase as a quasi-independent mini-studio (1998–2002). The innovative work of its Independent Film and Video Department was succeeded by the FilmFour Lab, and more recently the digital initiative Film4.0 has continued to provide development finance and practical support for low-budget independent film-making. The changing landscape of multi-channel digital television has also seen Channel 4 re-launch its subscription service FilmFour as Film4 on the digital terrestrial television platform Freeview, making it the only free-to-air dedicated film channel in the UK. Over the past 30 years, the intervention of television has transformed British film culture, not only in the 'hidden' practices of production investment and talent development, but conspicuously in cinemas, on TV screens and via DVD and video on demand (VoD). Arguably digital developments in the wider media ecology have, if anything, made television's multi-faceted contributions to screen culture more pronounced than ever.

The reality of the interdependence between film and television in the UK has been the *raison d'être* of a four-year project, 'Channel 4 and British Film Culture', funded by the Arts and Humanities Research Council (AHRC). The project team was based at the University of Portsmouth and worked in partnership with the British Universities Film and Video Council (BUFVC). This project proceeded from the revisionist perspective that a comprehensive understanding of film culture in the UK over the past 30 years is not possible without an appreciation of the crucial role played by television. It was the purpose of the project to assess the contribution of Channel 4 to British film culture in both economic and cultural terms. Moreover, it adopted a dual approach which considered not only Film4's production activities, but also its role as a broadcaster of a wide range of film content and programmes about film. It has thus considered not only the role of television in film culture, but also the place of film in television culture.

This dynamic relationship was identified in a 1987 article about the UK's then new fourth channel, published in German in the journal *Media Perspektiven*. The article has been translated by Corina Holzherr under the auspices of the Portsmouth project and is published in English here for the first time. Its authors, Gabriele Bock and Siegfried Zielinski, had conducted an investigation into Channel 4's origins and operation during its first four years, motivated by an interest in its unusual position as a commercially funded public service broadcaster. The article assesses the strengths and weaknesses of Channel 4's commissioning structure and identifies significant examples of its innovative programming, paying particular attention to its support for independent film. That emphasis is particularly noteworthy since it was West German television's film-funding mechanism that provided the model on which *Film on Four* was based. Through extensive policy research, interviews with many of the channel's pioneers and schedule analysis, the authors raised an important question about whether Channel 4's progressive public service remit could survive the commercial impetus of an expanding television market. The identification of that tension was prescient indeed, and it is a theme which runs through the subsequent contributions to this special issue.

Ieuan Franklin focuses on two British films of the 1980s which have fallen into obscurity. He uses the case studies of the bi-racial buddy/road movies *Fords on Water* (1983) and *Coast to Coast* (1987), funded by the BFI/Channel 4 and BBC respectively, to explore a number of factors that shaped film and television culture in the early to mid-1980s. These included: the importance of the television funding of feature films in an increasingly costly climate; the shifting strategic priorities of both the British Film Institute and the BBC during a pivotal moment in the history of their film-making activities; and the issues and difficulties involved in finding the right balance, in the 'television film', between social or political critique and comedy and generic conventions.

Forgotten films (as well as those most frequently recalled) are at the centre of Laura Mayne's investigation of canon formation in relation to Film4 films. She assesses the criteria by which a select number of films supported by Channel 4 have come to stand as typical in the minds of academics, critics and audiences, at the expense of others which have been neglected. Her article also considers Channel 4's role in constructing its own film canon through retrospective seasons tied to notable anniversaries, and highlights the commercial (as well as the cultural) factors behind the channel's ability to exploit extra value from its film back catalogue through DVD labels and VoD.

Justin Smith's contribution explores the tensions between Channel 4's ambitious and eclectic seasons of international art-house films and censorial pressures from policy-makers and lobbyists. The 'red triangle' experiment of 1986–7 deployed an on-screen warning symbol which was trialled in a season of controversial films and later abandoned after an inquest by the Independent Broadcasting Authority. Drawing policy lessons from that historical example, the article reflects on the comparative lack of adventure and curatorial imagination now evident in broadcast film provision in the multi-channel television market.

Broadcast film policy and scheduling is also the province of Rachael Keene's research, which analyses the shift in programming policy that took place when Channel 4's specialist subscription channel FilmFour was re-launched as Film4 on Freeview during 2006. By contrast with the thrust of some of the earlier contributions, Keene finds that while commercial imperatives were indeed a key factor in this evolution, Film4's scheduling strategies are also shown to be a product of the broadcaster's desire to reassert its public service identity in the multi-channel marketplace.

Tensions between a public service remit and commercial imperatives were evident at Channel 4's conception, and they have not gone away. They have persisted and been continually redefined as Channel 4 negotiated the fundamental structural changes that have taken place in the UK's television landscape over the past three decades. As those dynamics have shaped Channel 4's production and broadcasting commitments for film, then exploring these tensions through the lens of feature film reveals as much about television as it does about film. It is fitting that this special issue therefore concludes with an interview dossier drawn from our conversations with the four executives who have, since 1982, been successively responsible for commissioning films at Channel 4. Their testimony not only furnishes us with a unique narrative of that history from those who made it happen, it also reveals how Film4 has managed, in balancing creative freedom and commercial pressures, to develop a robust brand identity predicated on defending the principle of cultural subsidy for British film.

Acknowledgements

The editors gratefully acknowledge the support of the Arts and Humanities Research Council in sponsoring the research which has made possible this issue of the *Journal of British Cinema and Television*. The project team wishes to thank Channel 4 for their cooperation in completing this research, and in particular Rosie Gleeson, Information and Archives Manager, for her support and advice.

Arts & Humanities
Research Council

References

Department for Culture, Media and Sport (2012), *A Future for British Film: It Begins with the Audience*, London: DCMS.

Houston, P. (ed.) with Hassan, M., Puttnam, D., Isaacs, J., Perry, S., Millar, G., Bennett, A. and Parker, A. (1984), 'British cinema: life before death on television?', *Sight and Sound*, 53: 2, Spring, pp. 115–22.

Justin Smith is Reader in British Film Culture at the University of Portsmouth, UK. He is the author of *Withnail and Us: Cult Films and Film Cults in British Cinema* (2010) and, with Sue Harper, *British Film Culture in the 1970s: The Boundaries of Pleasure* (2011). He was Principal Investigator on the AHRC-funded project 'Channel 4 Television and British Film Culture' (2010–14) and is co-editor (with Paul McDonald) of its 2013 research output in the *Historical Journal of Film, Radio and Television*, 33:3.

Paul McDonald is Professor of Cinema and Media Industries at the University of Nottingham. He was Co-investigator for the project 'Channel 4 Television and British Film Culture'. He is the author of *Hollywood Stardom* (2013), *Video and DVD Industries* (2007) and *The Star System: Hollywood's Production of Popular Identities* (2000), and co-editor of *The Contemporary Hollywood Film Industry* (2008).

Britain's Channel 4: A TV Provider Caught Between Private Sector Funding and Its Cultural Mission

Gabriele Bock and Siegfried Zielinski
(translated by Corina Holzherr)

Abstract:

This article, which first appeared in *Media Perspektiven* 1 (1987), is published here for the first time in English. It offers an enlightening contemporary perspective, from the then German Federal Republic, on the innovation in European broadcasting which Channel 4 represented. It outlines the policy context which gave rise to the UK's fourth television channel and describes its unique, hybrid character as a commercial station funded by advertising revenue with a public service remit. It assesses the strengths and weaknesses of Channel 4's commissioning structure and identifies significant examples of its innovative programming, paying particular attention to its support for independent film. That emphasis is noteworthy since it was West German television's film-funding mechanism that provided the model on which *Film on Four* was based. The article recognises Channel 4's commitment to catering for minority audiences, to enabling broader access to programme-making and to commissioning work that was experimental in form and content. It is generous in suggesting that such a risk-taking cultural enterprise was only possible within the UK's mature and highly developed broadcasting ecology, but it remains cautious (perhaps presciently) of its sustainability in the expanding commercial marketplace of multi-channel television.

Keywords: Channel 4; IBA; ITV; OBA; programming; public service remit; publisher-broadcaster; schedules.

Journal of British Cinema and Television 11.4 (2014): 418–439
Edinburgh University Press
DOI: 10.3366/jbctv.2014.0227
© *Journal of British Cinema and Television*
www.euppublishing.com/jbctv

Introduction

On 2 November 1986 the fourth terrestrial channel in British television celebrated its anniversary. Four years previously, it had started broadcasting under the insignia of a computer-animated figure 4 – under close scrutiny from its national rivals as well as specialists from the international broadcasting industry. In an article published in *Media Perspektiven* 4 (1983), Stephen Hearst, then special adviser to the programming department and subsequently to the Director General of the BBC, predicted slim chances of success for this pioneer TV channel. Hearst felt that there were few development opportunities for the new channel, especially given the limited availability of financial and personnel resources (in its first year, there was, on average, a mere £30,000 available for each hour of programming). He also felt that the channel's core programming concept was wrong: 'In my opinion, television is too expensive for addressing small minorities, unless it also attempts to capture the interest and gain the favour of a wider public' (1983: 192).

In the recently published Peacock Report, which was primarily concerned with the future funding of the BBC, one recommendation (which was little more than a footnote) also addressed the funding of Channel 4: 'Channel 4 should be given the option of selling its own advertising time and would then no longer be funded by subscription from ITV companies' (Home Office 1986: 144).

But how compatible with each other are Stephen Hearst's rather sceptical prognosis and the recommendation to leave Channel 4 to the mercies of the free market economy? Is there not – as is often proposed in Germany – an irreconcilable contradiction between TV as a commercial enterprise and the progressive development of TV culture? And if commerce and culture are to be accommodated under the same roof, are they not inevitably in conflict?

The creation of Channel 4

Let's go back in time for a moment. In Germany, few know how Channel 4, a pioneer in the world of television, came into being and how it has since developed. And it is this lack of knowledge that tends to lead to premature calls for importing this 'ideal model' into, for instance, the German broadcasting service.

The Broadcasting Act, passed under the Conservative government in 1980, was the result of an intensive debate during the 1970s (which generated some brilliant innovative proposals) about reorganising the

British broadcasting landscape: Channel Four Television Company Ltd was inaugurated and – in January 1981 – started preparations for going on air.

Since the mid-1950s, UK television has been financed from two sources: the BBC as a public service is financed by the licence fees paid by television consumers; commercial television broadcasting, in the shape of the ITV companies, is financed by the sale of advertising. It is important to note, however, that this kind of commercial television is a 'special case' so to speak, that is its programming and advertising are under the supervision of a public body, the Independent Broadcasting Authority (IBA), which also gives out licences to private providers.

Technically, it has been possible to broadcast on four national television channels since the 1960s in Britain. However, having already awarded to the BBC the third terrestrial TV frequency (BBC2 started in April 1964) and local radio frequencies in 1963, Parliament would not have voted to give the BBC yet another national TV channel. Moreover, the BBC had their hands full providing programmes for their allocated frequencies and thus had no spare finances for expansion. Using the context of the debate around Channel 4, advertisers sought to break the private ITV companies' monopoly of TV advertising, proposing that BBC1 should also finance itself through advertising, while BBC2 and a newly established ITV2 should be relegated to the 'cultural ghettos'. These proposals were, however, unsuccessful. In the end, two viable but contrasting proposals came through as the only realistic options. Both took as their starting point the view that the BBC had to remain – in its status and existing rights – as it was:

1. Channel 4 was to be organised entirely innovatively, acting as a kind of 'publisher' (rather than a producer) and being a conduit for a wide range of voices. Programmes were to be sourced from companies, groups and institutions which were independent of the two existing television networks and were to serve hitherto neglected audiences. Most of all, as expressed in the Annan Report's proposal for creating an Open Broadcasting Authority (OBA), Channel 4 was to 'contribute something new and do it in a new way' (Home Office 1977: 472). On the principle of wide–ranging and balanced content, the most creative ideas were to be gathered. The finances were to come from block advertising, sponsored programmes and profit surpluses from the ITV companies. Such organisational and political solutions were strongly supported by independent British film-makers,

collectively represented by the Independent Filmmakers Association (IFA, which has since changed its name to IFVPA and
includes video and photography producers).

2. It was not only the Conservatives who were against the idea of
an OBA. The ITV companies were keen on claiming Channel
4 for themselves (in the interest of balancing the duopoly) as
a second ITV network, controlled by the IBA, financed from
advertising, and intended as a counterpart to BBC2.

In the relatively liberal early Thatcher era, in 1979–80, a compromise was finally reached, resulting in a somewhat risky symbiosis
between public and private, institutionalising Channel 4 as a living
contradiction:

- Channel 4 came under the control of the IBA, which is responsible
  for all private broadcasting in Great Britain, and Channel 4
  Television Company Ltd was nominated as a wholly owned
  subsidiary.
- The ITV companies were obliged to finance the new channel
  from surpluses of their (heavily taxed) advertising revenues. The
  tax burden of the ITV companies was thereby reduced. The ITV
  companies were given the right to sell advertising time on the
  new Channel 4. (As with ITV generally, this amounts to up to six
  minutes of advertising per hour of broadcasting.)
- With the exception of Wales, for which a special arrangement
  was reached, the new channel was conceived as a fourth national
  network, intended to offer a full programme.[1]
- The 'publisher' idea was by and large adhered to. With the exception of a regular 30-minute programme of audience feedback
  (*Right to Reply*), Channel 4 was not allowed to produce any programmes in-house. Instead, it was obliged to purchase most of its
  programmes from within the British market, plus a small number (15 per cent) from abroad. The ITV companies were also to
  produce programmes for Channel 4 (and thereby make full use of
  their capacities). All 'news' programmes had to be obtained from
  their common subsidiary ITN (Independent Television News
  Limited). Above all, a substantial proportion of the programming (though nowhere specified as a quota) was to come from
  the so-called independents of the British film and video scene – a
  dazzling array of companies and commercial producers, ranging
  from 'frustrated entrepreneurs' (Hood 1980: 81) at the fringes of
  the two established networks to radical alternative groups.

- Channel 4's programming brief was closely linked to the above 'publisher' idea: cultural and ethnic minorities – groups whose communicative needs had hitherto not been sufficiently taken account of – were to be reached and to be given a voice. A minimum of 15 per cent of broadcasting time was thus allocated for educational programmes and a minimum of 60 minutes per week for broadcasts with religious content. Finally, Channel 4 was to contribute to a renewal of television culture and televisual forms, even though the necessary experimental broadcasts were not expected always to secure a mass audience.

In Germany, we are not unfamiliar with such projections. The third ARD programmes went on air under similar auspices. Channel 4 is different in that it is a private provider with a public mandate. Given that the BBC and ITV had hitherto produced themselves all the material that they didn't purchase abroad, the requirement for strict separation between editorial responsibility and programme production was downright revolutionary in Britain. Moreover, the obligation on Channel 4 to purchase its programmes from third parties fitted nicely into the economic-political ideas of the Thatcher government in that it was going to promote small and medium enterprises within the British audiovisual sector.

Without responsibility for production, which inevitably requires administrative organisation, Channel 4 is able to work with a minimal number of personnel (which does, however, lead to chronic and extreme stress levels, according to staff members). In 1985–6, the operation of its national network was carried by only 246 staff which meant that most of its budget, amounting to 88.5 per cent in 1985–6, could be invested in programming (Channel Four Television Company Ltd 1986). By comparison, the BBC has 30,000 employees in total. The share that Channel 4 receives from advertising by the ITV companies was determined on a percentage basis (between 14 per cent and 18 per cent). The advantage of such an arrangement is that its budget increases in line with an increase in advertising revenues. Currently, Channel 4 receives 17 per cent of the net income of the ITV companies, 20 per cent of which goes to the Welsh S4C. This leaves Channel 4 with a budget of £135.8 million for the financial year 1986–7 (compared to approximately £80 million when it first started). This means that a good £120 million can flow into independent film production as well as into the purchase of programmes.

It was clear from the start that the ITV companies were not going to subsidise Channel 4 in the long-term. After all, it was the British state that was going to lose out on additional revenue from the special tax levied on the high advertising revenues from commercial television. A year before Channel 4's launch, Jeremy Isaacs made the following forecast: 'If Channel 4 is able to win our predicted share of at least 10 per cent of overall television audiences, there is no doubt in my mind that the ITV companies ... will not only get their money back, but may earn additional revenue by the advertising they sell during our hours of broadcasting' (1981: 587).

We will now take a closer look at what Channel 4's programming actually looks like, occupying a position between the established broadcasting providers, advanced technologies for TV distribution and ventures in video recording (a medium that is particularly popular in Great Britain).

Programming structure

With a brief to provide a wide-ranging full-time broadcasting service, it was clear from the start that Channel 4 had a difficult task to fulfil. Not only did it have to serve those groups – mainly minorities – that other TV providers had been neglecting, but it was going to broadcast a full 60 hours per week from the word go. By now, just over four years after its inception, broadcasting hours have increased to an average of over 70 hours per week and are set to continue rising.

On weekdays, Channel 4 starts broadcasting in the early afternoon, while at weekends programmes start around lunchtime. Daily broadcasting stops shortly after midnight. In fact, Channel 4 programming is highly flexible: the start and the end of a day of broadcasting can, for instance, vary according to the timing of special sporting events or transmissions from Parliamentary proceedings. Four times a year, the sequence of programmes is publicly announced at the so-called 'Launches'. This means that structural changes, such as shifting regular features to different broadcasting slots, are possible at relatively short notice.

The overall aim of any broadcasting plan is to schedule regularly reoccurring programmes at fixed times. That said, Channel 4 programming is characterised by a high proportion of programmes of variable length (such as films, operas, ballets). Therefore, the starting times of the regular programmes will often vary and the programming schedule may appear somewhat 'restless' (cf. Table 1).

Our analysis of the programming content revealed that Channel 4 prioritises films, with nine featuring in the weekly edition of the *TV Times* that we had selected.[2] The number of films and the mix

423

Table 1. Overview of Channel 4 programmes for the week
11 October–17 October 1986

Time	Saturday	Sunday	Monday	Tuesday	Wednesday	Thursday	Friday
13.00	Channel 4	Baseball					
13.30	Racing						
14.00		Everybody Here					
14.30		They Got	The Late	Down	Buck	Channel 4	Channel 4
15.00	Angels Wash	Me Covered (1943)	Late Show	Memory Lane (1951)	Privates (1941)	Racing	Racing
15.30	Their Faces		The Irish Angle	10 Million			
16.00	(1939)	This Made News	Mavis on 4		Mavis on 4		
16.30	Le Pèlerinage		Countdown	Countdown	Countdown	Countdown	Countdown
17.00	(1961)	Sir Peter Scott					
17.30	Brookside omnibus	News sum. Business Programme	Grampian Sheepdog Trials	Bewitched Make It Pay	Hogan's Heroes Abbott and Costello	Those Marvellous Benchley Shorts	Car 54, Where Are You? Solid Soul The Chart Show
18.00	Right to Reply	American Football	I Could Do That	Keeping Your Words	Family Ties		
18.30	Boat Race		Write On	Ellis Island Show	In Time of War	Union World	
19.00	News 7 Days		Channel 4 News	Channel 4 News	Channel 4 News	Channel 4 News	Channel 4 News
19.30	Strangers Abroad	Chasing Rainbows	Comment Weather	Comment Weather	Comment Weather	Comment Weather	Weather Book choice
20.00		Fish Out of Water	Brookside	Brookside	Talking to Writers	Equinox Shock	What the Papers Say/A
20.30	Redbrick		Fairly Secret Army	Wild Screen Awards	Diverse Reports	Trauma	Week in Politics
21.00	Paradise Postponed	Baryshnikov by Tharp	St. Elsewhere	1986	Werther	Oh Madeline	The Cosby Show
21.30			4 Minutes			Annika	Gardeners' Calendar
22.00	Hill Street		Oil: The	Kiss Me			Golden Girls
22.30	Blues	Wuthering Heights	Independ- ents	Goodbye (1982)		Going for Gold	Living with Schizophrenia
23.00	Saturday Almost	(1939)	The Eleventh		La Vie à l'Envers		
23.30	Live		Hour. Scorpio		(1964)	Beyond Belief	Identification of a Woman (1982)
24.00	Ministry of Fear		Rising/What Can I Do	Too Close for Comfort		Relative Strangers	
0.30	(1943)		with a Male Nude/17				
1.00			Rooms				

Source: TV Times.

of old and new films during that week can be regarded as typical
for Channel 4. Another focus is on series – again a mix of old and
new – including cheap imports from the USA (for example *Bewitched* or
Too Close for Comfort) and *Brookside*, a series specifically commissioned

by Channel 4 four years ago and intended as a counterpart to ITV's *Coronation Street*. The idea behind *Brookside* was to address – through fiction – issues affecting British society, such as unemployment, the dual burden of work and family on women or inadequate parenting.[3]

Compared to Channel 4's first full broadcasting week in November 1982, the week of 11–17 October 1986 revealed twice the amount of fictional series (seventeen), as well as a repeat of *Brookside* on Saturday. To conclude from this fact alone that programming is more 'commercial' nowadays would, nevertheless, be hasty. It is important to analyse Channel 4 programming over a longer period – only then is it possible to detect certain trends. Among their more 'unusual series' were, for instance, the two Brazilian productions *Dancin' Days* and *Slave Girls Isaura*; the latter had recently also been broadcast in one of ARD's afternoon slots.[4]

In addition to the distribution of broadcasting times for series and films, Table 2 shows that on weekdays, the news is the only steady and constant feature in the entire programme. Both the scope and the timing of the news have remained constant since Channel 4 started, with the only exception that in the beginning, the Friday news was only half an hour long. The Friday news has since been extended and brought in line with the news length on other weekdays. Furthermore, news summaries have been introduced at weekends. The overview of Table 2 also shows those broadcasts that are particularly characteristic for Channel 4. A comparison of Tables 1 and 2 reveals that the blank spaces left in Table 2 are shown in Table 1 as documentaries, information broadcasts, cultural programmes, shows and quizzes.

It suffices to look at Channel 4's proportional programming types within an average week to realise that it is different from other commercial and non-commercial television broadcasters (Table 3). Non-fiction programmes count for an unusually high share of over 40 per cent. Almost 20 per cent of the entire broadcasting time is dedicated to 'current affairs and general factuals', with the addition of news, educational programmes and other documentaries, some of the latter referring to current issues. In the financial year 1984–5, 35 per cent of programming was dedicated to fiction: films, serials and drama series.

In our representative edition of the *TV Times*, out of 75 broadcasting hours, 27 hours are dedicated to series and films (36 per cent). This corresponds almost exactly to the average weekly quota cited in the IBA yearbook 1986. Even the addition of the 30-minute French short film *Le Pèlerinage* (1961) does not substantially increase this share. Three short films (from the *Eleventh Hour*) were considered

Table 2. Overview of films, serials, drama series, sports programmes and in-house programmes in the week 11 October–17 October 1986*

Time	Saturday	Sunday	Monday	Tuesday	Wednesday	Thursday	Friday
12.30							
13.00		Sport					
13.30	Sport						
14.00							
14.30							
15.00	Film (1939)	Film (1943)		Film (1951)	Film (1941)	Sport	Sport
15.30							
16.00							
16.30							
17.00	C4 series (rpt. from Monday and Tuesday)	News sum.					
17.30				Series	Series		Series
18.00							Youth programme
18.30	*Right to Reply*	Sport			Series		
19.00	Sport				Series		Pop music
19.30	News sum.		Channel 4 News Comment Weather	Channel 4 News Comment Weather	Channel 4 News Comment Weather	Channel 4 News Comment Weather	Channel 4 News Weather
20.00							
20.30			C4 series	C4 series			
21.00			Series		Current affairs		
21.30							

non-classifiable borderline programmes between documentary and fiction and were thus left out.

Apart from a high proportion of non-fiction and flexible programming, the programming structure of Channel 4 does not appear to be particularly innovative. The large proportion of cheap fiction imports from the US may well disappoint those who expected an 'alternative' broadcasting service from Channel 4, but 75 hours of weekly broadcasting does, of course, not come cheap. However, a closer look reveals an innovative element in Channel 4 programming

Table 2. Continued.

Time	Saturday	Sunday	Monday	Tuesday	Wednesday	Thursday	Friday
22.00	ITV series (rpt.)		Series			Series	Series
22.30							
23.00	Series		4 Minutes			Series (formerly on ITV)	
23.30		Film (1939)		Film (1982)	Film (1964)		
24.00			Eleventh Hour				Series
0.30							
1.00							Film (1982)
		Film (1943)		Series		Series	

*Table 2 shows only those broadcasts that occur frequently or routinely in those particular slots. A comparison of Tables 1 and 2 reveals that the blank spaces left in Table 2 are shown in Table 1 as documentaries, information broadcasts, sophisticated cultural programmes, shows and quizzes. For certain programmes, especially for commissions by Channel 4, it is difficult to match them with traditional programming genres.

Translator's note: In German the word 'Serie' refers to both serial and series, so 'Series' in the table above may refer to either.

that is less quantifiable: an effort appears to have been made across programme types to find both new types of programmes and new and innovative content.

Special features of the non-fiction programme

From the beginning, Channel 4 has had the brief to be innovative both in form and content across programme types. This posed a particular challenge for the areas of general TV news, political news programmes and documentaries, where other providers had already extensively experimented with the format of reports and other presentations.

Channel 4 has from the start been obliged to buy in its news programmes as well as all other programmes from outside (except for *Right to Reply*). In the beginning, after an intensive search on the free market, Channel 4 was unable to find a production company with sufficient capacity to produce news programmes. Eventually, with the agreement of the IBA, it commissioned the company that produced

Table 3. Average weekly broadcasting according to types of programmes (figures for one average week in the financial year ending 31 March 1985)

	Duration in hoursand minutes	Share inper cent
News	4.00	6
Current affairs and general documentaries	13.05	19
Art	2.40	4
Religion	1.15	2
Learning and education	7.29	11
Sub-total of information programmes	28.29	42
Teleplays, serials and drama series	14.45	21
Feature films	9.33	14
Sub-total of different types of 'stories'	24.18	35
Entertainment and music	11.13	16
Sport	5.01	7
Total of all programmes	69.01	100

Source: IBA (1986).

the news programmes for the ITV companies, Independent Television News (ITN), with the production of its news.

ITN has a team of approximately 120 staff to take sole care of the *Channel 4 News* programmes; these include five news broadcasts of almost 60 minutes on weekdays (interrupted by two advertising slots) and two shorter versions of news at the weekend. These programmes are delivered to Channel 4 in the same way as the films and documentaries, which means that Channel 4 has neither a say in its design nor is in a position to respond to any given events that may come up at short notice.

Apart from the longer duration of the news programmes, which allow for the inclusion of several as well as longer contributions to one topic, Channel 4 news does not significantly differ from ITV or BBC news: it is quite conventional in nature, structure and presentation with no signs of innovative experimentation. In terms of content, however, *Channel 4 News* is innovative in so far as its focus has shifted away from 'headline journalism'.

Since the news teams have more time at their disposal, they are able to describe the background of and developments around events.

Furthermore, in stark contrast to other providers, Channel 4 focuses on specific topics such as science, technology, art or economics. Even the Royal Family is given less attention by Channel 4. While the wedding of Prince Andrew and Sarah Ferguson took up almost the entire duration of the BBC and ITV news, Channel 4 settled for a brief mention after the first advertising break. A similar disregard is exercised for the reporting of natural disasters and criminal acts of violence.

While Channel 4 has virtually no influence over the design of the news programmes, it does choose its own commentators, who – from Mondays to Thursdays after the news – give their opinion on certain events. The original intention was to give a voice to a manageable number of representatives from differing social groups, but to date over 700 well–known or lesser-known personalities have been given the opportunity to contribute. This may be seen as testimony to a relative openness on the part of Channel 4. In the week selected for this article, the following individuals were commenting in this slot: the president of the Institute of Public Relations, a representative of the Eritrean Information Service, a Member of Parliament, and Peter Bull, who was introduced by the *TV Times* as a 'former nurse and self-employed builder'.[5]

Channel 4 News is always closely connected to the channel's many current affairs programmes. A prime example is the magazine programme *Bandung File*, relating to and aimed at ethnic minorities. Its editor Farrukh Dhondy pursues the following objectives:

- to give an opportunity to ethnic minorities to present themselves and issues relating to their lives to a wider public through the medium of TV;
- to inform these minorities on a regular basis about social issues in the countries of their own or their forefathers' origin.

Each programme consists of a selection of topical issues plus a roughly 20-minute documentary, which may relate to a third-world country or address the living conditions of minorities in cities like, for instance, Birmingham. Independent film and video producers provide Dhondy with contributions towards his programme (Dhondy 1986). The producers are often themselves members of the minority they report on, which is why their programmes tend to have a very authentic flavour.

Friday Alternative is another example of a Channel 4 programme on topical issues. Slotted in after the 30–minute news on Friday, this pioneering current affairs show – characterised by a radically new reporting style and aimed primarily at a younger audience – soon made Channel 4 history. It consisted of a dynamic mix of relatively short reports presented from a range of perspectives. Accompanying state-of-the-art computer graphics and video animations (a video artist was co-producer) ensured that the reports became accessible to all viewers.

One of its early broadcasts scrutinised the government's claim that inflation and unemployment rates were linked and that the government's prioritisation for bringing down inflation rather than unemployment was justified. The programme used computer graphics to show how unemployment and inflation had actually developed over a long period and that the linkage between the two was not as obvious as had been claimed by the British government.

Friday Alternative was produced by a company called Diverse Productions, headed by former BBC employee David Graham. In order to make the programme as lively as possible, both in terms of content and format, 240 people from 20 different groups were recruited from all over the country, each contributing from their unique perspective. Yet it was precisely this enriching new dimension of diversity that brought about the downfall of the programme. A story dealing with media reporting on the Falklands war by the British media was taken as grounds for accusing *Friday Alternative* for lack of professionalism. In the end, the programme was quietly removed from the timetable over the summer break.

Diverse Productions was then commissioned to develop a new programme and, after six months, came up with *Diverse Reports*, a series that is still being broadcast today. The groups that had contributed to *Friday Alternative* were dissolved, the computer graphics were scrapped and experienced journalists were hired to assure professional standards. First, the programme contained several reports of a certain length, but nowadays the focus is on a single topic per programme. The only difference between *Diverse Reports* and conventional magazine programmes is that it has a different conception of balance. Opinion journalism is still practised and equilibrium of the perspective is upheld across the entirety of the programmes rather than within one single programme. According to David Graham, the deciding factor for the selection of a topic is not its political stance but its unusual perspective.[6]

Investment in independent audiovisual culture

In 1985–6, a quarter of Channel 4 programmes, amounting to 43 per cent of its budget, came from the independent sector (Channel Four Television Company 1986). They were mainly 'specials' and serials of the type described above and spanned a wide range of topics from art programmes to current affairs. Nonetheless, two strands of programmes – deliberately created by Channel 4 and particularly relevant to the British film and video industry – can be identified. The *Eleventh Hour* and *People to People* are series overseen by Alan Fountain as commissioning editor, while *Film on Four* is a series of mainly original films and dramas. Behind the choice of these three programmes is the intention to promote culture in two very different ways and a large part of Channel 4's international recognition as an innovative broadcaster is due to the inclusion of these programmes.

Eleventh Hour and *People to People* are typical examples of Channel 4's addressing and representing audiences that have hitherto been neglected or entirely left out. These slots now provide audiovisual producers (like the independent film-makers who earlier fought for the 'publisher concept') with opportunities to create their own programmes. They include a range of producers and experimentalists in video and cine film as well as some quite radical political groups, who all share a sense of disapproval of established television culture and aesthetics.

Programmes for these strands are predominantly produced in workshops, most of which have sprung up in a number of British regions over the last few years, but some of which were established a decade and a half ago (for example Amber Films). They are financed by communal and regional policies that promote culture, and supported by trade unions, by the British Film Institute (BFI) and occasionally by private sponsors. As production collectives, film or video distributors or operators of production studios, they are thus independent of the broadcasters. In this area of programme production, Channel 4's approach is different from the rest of independent film production in that instead of commissioning individual programmes, it promotes the overall work of a workshop. A workshop will, for instance, receive funding for up to three years. In return, Channel 4 is able to select programmes for television broadcasting from the pool of the workshop's productions, while the workshop retains the right additionally to exploit its productions for other purposes. In principle, the funding is granted independently of whether or not the workshop productions are selected for television screening.

In this way, Channel 4 undertakes to promote the entire workshop endeavour, thereby giving a kind of infrastructural support to workshops (it also helps with setting up new groups), or in Alan Fountain's words, 'the self-contained existence of independent film and video production companies is of prime interest to Channel 4 as a source for innovative and experimental programmes' (Fountain et al. 1986: 3). Currently, Channel 4 is supporting four workshops on a three-year basis and a further ten on one-year contracts. Business development funds go to another four workshops and so-called 'resource funding' is given to another five workshops, amounting to a total of 23 workshops in receipt of Channel 4 financing. Additionally, Channel 4 has been supporting a further fourteen workshops since its launch four years ago.

The promotion of feature films

In terms of established genre categories, *Eleventh Hour* and *People to People* would come under documentaries, although many of the more recent productions are characterised by a distinct blurring of boundaries between fact and fiction. These innovative productions have been brought into British television by independent British film-makers who have freed themselves from the restraints of programme compartmentalisation.

To the outside world, the promotion of feature films is mainly taken care of by *Film on Four* under the direction of David Rose, who joined Channel 4 with 25 years' experience within drama at the BBC. This strand of programming approximately equates to the impact that the 'Film/Fernsehabkommen' (agreement for government funding of film production) has had for years on the infrastructure of German film production. The relatively steep rise in British film production since the beginning of the 1980s, coupled with a simultaneous decline in cinema attendance and the fact that 'New British Cinema' has become a trademark at international film festivals in recent years, are all closely linked to the role that Channel 4 has played (Docherty et al. 1985). Set up in spring 1984 with the international film market in mind, Channel 4 and Film Four International (FFI) have become a focal point for the British and West European film scene. And Channel 4 films, which can also be shown in cinemas, have become something of a centre of gravity within Channel 4 programming.

Apart from the dedicated contributions by the many enthusiastic staff members of Channel 4 (the role of Deputy Chairman on the Board of Directors is currently the director, producer and president of Goldcrest Films Limited, Sir Richard Attenborough), its success in promoting feature films is largely due to the fact that editorial responsibility and audiovisual production are strictly separated. Together with a brief for innovative content, such a separation enables Channel 4 to invest a large part of its budget in creative independent film and television production. Up to the autumn of 1986, this amounted to a yearly average of £8–10 million, invested in a total of 107 productions (Channel Four Television Company 1986).

The different means and strategies employed for the promotion of films are testimony to a highly creative Channel 4 management team. Given this diversity in approach, it is often hard for the outsider to identify those programmes to which Channel 4 has contributed:

- First of all, there are the commissions that Channel 4 undertakes on the basis of project proposals and scripts received. In the beginning, Channel 4's relatively meagre budget was divided up evenly to assist the 20 productions per year, but this inevitably led to low-budget productions. Over time, more complex co-financing models have been adopted, with substantial contributions by Channel 4 and in particular with a higher allocation of funds to particular films. In terms of quantity, so far 20 productions have been entirely financed by Channel 4 and another 47 have been co-financed (the other 40 productions in *Film on Four* consisted of 28 pre-purchased productions, ten repeats from ITV and two 'licensed' films).

- Channel 4 has been and still is involved in first-class international co-productions, such as the Swiss/Portuguese film *Dans la ville blanche/In the White City* (1983) by Alain Tanner and *Paris, Texas* (1984) for which Wim Wenders received financial backing in exchange for the rights to *Flight to Berlin* (1983) (Isaacs, in Houston et al. 1984: 118).

- Through Film Four International, Channel 4 can sell feature films that it has financed or co-financed. In turn, the proceeds from FFI films have gone, over the last two years, into the production of such outstanding films as *A Zed and Two Noughts* (1985) by Peter Greenaway, *Letter to Brezhnev* (1985) by Chris Bernard and *My Beautiful Laundrette* (1985) by Stephen Frears.

- Channel 4's close cooperation with the BFI is crucial in the context of the British film industry. It includes distribution as well as production. In 1986, for instance, the two institutions, equipped with a selection of films from the 1985 London Film Festival, went on tour, visiting thirteen British cities. The current annual BFI yearbook proudly acknowledges the receipt of a generous financial contribution by Channel 4 for its feature film production activities over the next three years (British Film Institute 1986: 27). Because of the channel's support for the BFI's Production Board, each film that is produced over the last few years is indirectly also a Channel 4 film (for example *Caravaggio* (1986) by Derek Jarman, which cost a mere £475,000).

• Channel 4 repeatedly stepped into the breach in situations where outstanding films would have run out of funding during their production. This was the case with Greenaway's *The Draughtman's Contract* (1982) and Richard Eyre's *The Ploughman's Lunch* (1983). Channel 4's flexibility to come to the rescue spontaneously in such situations is possibly one of its most impressive characteristics.

The apparent loss of cinematic quality and the increasing substitution of the 'movie-movie' culture by a 'TV movie' culture has, over the last four years, been a constant concern vociferously expressed by film critics (Houston et al. 1984). However, with regard to the cinema screening of the films by Greenaway, Jarman, Jordan and Eyre, such criticism is hardly justified. Moreover, many directors have been making films for the small screen for years. And directors such as Peter Greenaway have long moved beyond the possibilities of cinema film; the videos he produced for Channel 4 are among the best and most innovative productions that have been achieved in audiovisual culture over the last few years.

A more pressing issue is the dependency relationship between Channel 4 and the independent film-makers. Against the background of Channel 4's position as the only important distributor of audiovisual material and as commissioner rather than producer, these small independent production companies, often established for the sole purpose of producing for Channel 4, rely heavily on Channel 4 for their existence. Moreover, the BBC and ITV will probably not change their production policies in the foreseeable future. This became particularly evident when proposals in the Peacock Report for an increase in commissions were met with a negative reaction by the BBC.

Acceptance

Even though Channel 4 is financed from the profits of the ITV companies and therefore does not depend on viewing figures, in the end it is the public – as well as the politicians in charge – who decide how successful Channel 4 is. The Channel 4 annual report of 1986 reveals that since November 1983 Channel 4's share in overall television viewing figures has steadily increased (Channel Four Television Company 1986). While ratings hovered between 4 per cent and 5 per cent initially (Hearst 1983: 194), by January 1986 they had risen to a monthly average of 9 per cent.

The weekly viewing figures have continually risen over the past four years (Wakshlag 1985). In early 1986, 90 per cent of households with a television viewed at least one Channel 4 programme per week. Viewer behaviour appears to reflect Channel 4's programming policies in relation to target groups: many choose those broadcasts that have been designed for them. The fact that people do not stay with one channel over a long period is reflected in the average daily viewing time of 18 minutes (ibid.: 23).

Along with rising numbers of viewers, the British people's attitude towards Channel 4 has changed too. By now, only a quarter of those questioned believe that it is aimed at minorities, while in 1983, almost 50 per cent thought so. Channel 4's image has become more positive and its difference from other broadcasters is perceived more clearly by the public: for example, its experimental approach, its new forms of programmes, distinctive content and the fact that many programmes are aimed at specific target groups and are not offered in the same form by any other provider (ibid.: 23).

In 1985, the IBA launched a large-scale survey (*Attitudes to Broadcasting*), the aim of which was to compare the programming schedule of all UK television providers. The question as to which channel provided the best programmes within individual programme categories yielded a surprising result for Channel 4. Forty-one per cent of respondents named youth programming for 16–24 year olds as the top category; within this category, 19 per cent of respondents favoured ITV and a remarkable 10 per cent favoured Channel 4. Channel 4 was thereby voted equally popular as BBC1 and far more popular than BBC2 (2 per cent). In the category of cinema films, Channel 4 also outscored BBC2 with 7 per cent versus 5 per cent, although the two large providers were clearly in the lead in this category (ITV: 33 per cent; BBC: 18 per cent) (IBA Research Department 1986: 10).

Summative comments – particularly in view of Channel 4 as a potential model for future channels

1. In its brief history, Channel 4 has to some extent proven that it is possible to appeal to a wide audience by, for instance, combining

within one single programme such contrasting contributions as the portrayal of minority groups alongside what might be called elite audiovisual computer graphics and video animations. Not least because of its limited financial resources (which primarily affect the entertainment segment aimed at appealing to a broad public) the result is a mixture of cheap imports, ITV repeats and experimental, creative and often highly ambitious programmes. Examples are arts programmes, feature films and video productions, themed mini-series and even such unprepossessing little slots as *Four Minutes*, in which an attempt is made to recapture for television short films that do not follow in the tradition of commercial video-clip culture.

2. Channel 4 does not function just as the IBA's cultural flagship for private television (in the IBA annual reports, a disproportionately large section is given over to the description of Channel 4 programmes), but there is a danger that its programmes aimed at minorities fulfil a kind of 'alibi' function for the ITV companies. In other words, Channel 4's regular broadcasting of programmes aimed at specific target groups such as ethnic minorities, religious groups, young people and trade union members relieves the ITV companies of their duty to make space in their schedules for the communicative concerns of those groups.

3. The complete separation of editing and production has undoubtedly had an effect on the infrastructure of British broadcasting culture and has, in particular, led to a renaissance in the production of independent films. But the downside is that the programmes are 'canned goods' in that they have mostly been produced in advance. It is thus only possible to report on national or international current affairs or react spontaneously to political or cultural events within the news broadcasts delivered by ITN. Diverse Productions, for instance, requires a production lead time of approximately five weeks for one of their 'report' programmes. Thus the reporting of and reacting to topical events falls exclusively to the BBC and ITV. Channel 4 therefore loses out on opportunities to experiment with live TV, which – against the background of the 'canned goods' offered by the new distributors such as cable and satellite TV and video recording – is becoming ever more central to TV output in general.

4. The abandonment of the idea of a mass audience in favour of attracting specific, often small, target groups with diverse

interests and tastes – frequently referred to by representatives of Channel 4 and in particular by its chief executive Jeremy Isaacs – has certainly instilled a progressive impetus into established television programming. But it does not come without risks. Such fragmented programming is also ideal for pay-TV and pay-per-view services and was in fact part of a long-term projection for the British television landscape proposed by the Peacock Committee (Hearst 1986).

5. At present, the 'Channel 4 experiment' is feasible only thanks to its niche existence within the established duopoly of the two large British television broadcasters. The BBC on the one hand, as the only broadcasting service for which the British people are willing to pay high licence fees, and ITV on the other hand, which – thanks to its monopoly on advertising – receives extremely high revenues, remain the two guarantors of a continuation of Channel 4's current programme profile. A change in this set-up would not only have important consequences for both the BBC and ITV, but also for Channel 4, which undoubtedly is one of the more remarkable innovations on the European television scene. A reduction in advertising revenue by the ITV companies, for example as a consequence of advertising coming into the BBC or of the emergence of viable commercial competitors, would take away the very livelihood of Channel 4. Its self-financing system through selling advertising slots would force it to become an ordinary competitor of the other ITV companies. In the long term, this would fatally compromise the current experimental culture and its commitment to minorities.

6. And finally, we would add a seemingly trivial consideration which is, however, relevant in terms of Channel 4's status as a model. The social sub-system 'television' is only one part of a complex overall social and historical system. The launch of Channel 4 was the result of a long and intensive political and cultural debate, which has inevitably shaped its current format. We believe that it is impossible to undertake such an experiment in a society that has no tradition of media-related political discourse such as has existed within the British broadcasting landscape since its beginnings in the 1920s. A final note on the feasibility of transferring an idea that is rooted in a particular – in this case uniquely British – culture: experimental or innovative programmes such as those that emerged under the direction of Michael Kustow,[7]

or the provocative elements of current affairs programmes such as *Opinions*, not only call for a high tolerance threshold on the part of the television audience, they also require more general support from a public for whom radical ways of addressing aesthetic and political issues are part and parcel of everyday life.

Acknowledgements

The editors are grateful to Professor Zielinski and to *Media Perspektiven* for permission to publish this translation, for which we are indebted to Corina Holzherr.

Notes

1. Sianel Pedwar Cymru (S4C).
2. *TV Times*, 11 October–17 October 1986. The Channel 4 Press Pack for that week's scheduled broadcasts is available at Channel 4 Press Packs, 'Cover: 1986 week 42 page 1'. See < http://bufvc.ac.uk/tvandradio/c4pp/search/index.php/page/c4_pp_1986_42_1011_1017_001_cover > (accessed 1 June 2014).
3. *TV Times*, 30 October–5 November 1982, pp. 84–6.
4. Arbeitsgemeinschaft der öffentlich-rechtlichen Rundfunkanstalten der Bundesrepublik Deutschland (ARD) is Germany's major consortium of regional public service broadcasters.
5. Quotation derived from Channel 4 Press Information Pack listings for Tuesday, 14 October 1986. Channel 4 Press Packs, 'Programme listings: 1986 week 42 page 64'. See < http://bufvc.ac.uk/tvandradio/c4pp/search/index.php/page/c4_pp_1986_42_1011_1017_064_proglist > (accessed 25 May 2014).
6. Comments made during the podium discussion at the Workshop on Channel 4 held under the auspices of the British Council at the Academy of Arts, Berlin, 26–29 November 1986.
7. Michael Kustow was Commissioning Editor for Arts Programmes at Channel 4, 1982–9.

References

British Film Institute (1986), *BFI Film and Television Yearbook 1986*, London: BFI Publishing.

Channel Four Television Company Ltd (1986), *Statistical Information*, London: Channel Four.

Dhondy, F. (1986), interview with the authors, 27 November.

Docherty, D., Morrison, D. and Tracey, M. (1985), 'The British film industry in the 1980s: the challenge of change', *Media Perspektiven*, 11, pp. 813–20.

Fountain, A., Stoneman, R. and Spry, C. (1986), *The Work of Channel Four's Independent Film and Video Department*, London: Channel Four.

Hearst, S. (1983), 'Broadcasting research in Great Britain', *Media Perspektiven*, 4, pp. 191–8.

Hearst, S. (1986), 'The Peacock Report: a critique', *Media Perspektiven*, 9, pp. 567–81.

Home Office (1977) *Report of the Committee on the Future of Broadcasting* (The Annan Report), London: HMSO.

Home Office (1986), *Report of the Committee on Financing the BBC* (The Peacock Report), London: HMSO.

Hood, S. (1980), *On Television*, London: Pluto.

Houston, P. (ed.) with Hassan, M., Puttnam, D., Isaacs, J., Perry, S., Millar, G., Bennett, A. and Parker, A. (1984), 'British cinema: life before death on television?', *Sight and Sound*, 53: 2, Spring, pp. 115–22.

IBA Research Department (1986), *Attitudes to Broadcasting in 1985*, London: Independent Broadcasting Authority.

Independent Broadcasting Authority (1986), *Television and Radio 1986: The IBA Yearbook of Independent Broadcasting*, London: Independent Broadcasting Authority.

Isaacs, J. (1981), 'The new Channel: in what ways will Channel 4 provide a distinctive service?', *The Listener*, 5 November, pp. 526–7.

Wakshlag, J. (1985), *Channel 4: The Audience's Response*, London: Independent Broadcasting Authority, IBA Research Department.

Gabriele Bock was a founding member of the Arbeitskreis Technische Kommunikation and post-doctoral researcher at the Technische Universität Berlin, Institut für Medienwissenschaft. Since 1995 she has run her own media consultancy. Her publications include: Friedrich Knilli, Knut Hickethier, Siegfried Zielinski and Gabriele Bock (eds), *Medien/Kultur: Schnittstellen zwischen Medienwissenschaft, Medienpraxis und gesellschaftlicher Kommunikation* (1991) and 'Abgestufte Nähe: Kooperation und Kommunikation im Büroalltag', in Stefan Beck (ed.), *Technogene Nähe. Ethnographische Studien zur Mediennutzung im Alltag* (2000).

Siegfried Zielinski is Chair in Media Theory: Archaeology and Variantology of the Media, Director of the International Vilém-Flusser-Archive at Berlin University of the Arts and Michel Foucault Professor for Techno-Culture and Media Archaeology at the European Graduate School in Saas Fee. He is the author of numerous publications including *Video – Apparat, Medium, Kunst, Kultur: Ein internationaler Reader* (1992), *Archäologie der Medien: Zur Tiefenzeit des technischen Hörens und Sehens* (2002), and co-editor, with Eckhard Fürlus, of *Variantology 5 – Neapolitan Affairs. On Deep Time Relations of Arts, Sciences and Technologies* (2010).

Roadblocks and Roads Not Taken: *Fords on Water* (1983), *Coast to Coast* (1987) and the British Bi-racial Buddy-Road Movie

Ieuan Franklin

Abstract:
This article is about two low-budget British road movies which have long disappeared from the cultural radar: *Fords on Water* (1983) and *Coast to Coast* (1987). These films will be used as case studies to explore a number of factors that shaped film and television culture in the early to mid-1980s, including the importance of the television funding of feature films in an increasingly costly climate; the shifting strategic priorities of both the British Film Institute and the BBC during a pivotal moment in the history of their film-making activities; and the issues and difficulties involved in finding the right balance between social or political critique and comedy and generic conventions. The two films are rare examples of what might be termed 'British bi-racial buddy-road movies'. The article will focus on the attributes they share: their obscurity and unavailability; their TV funding; their genre; and their theme of an inter-racial friendship bonded over a desire to escape from boredom and unemployment in Thatcher's Britain. However, it will also tease out their very different approaches, in terms of the more subtle and the more visceral aspects of tone, humour, politics and aesthetics. Finally, the article will consider the factors which prevented these lively films from reaching the wide audience they deserved, and whether they represent two 'roads not taken' in the intervening period in British film culture.

Keywords: 1980s; British Broadcasting Corporation; British Film Institute; Channel 4; comedy; genre; race; radicalism; realism; road movies; unemployment.

Journal of British Cinema and Television 11.4 (2014): 440–458
Edinburgh University Press
DOI: 10.3366/jbctv.2014.0228
© *Journal of British Cinema and Television*
www.euppublishing.com/jbctv

Introduction

This article is about two low-budget British road movies which have long disappeared from the cultural radar: *Fords on Water* (1983) and *Coast to Coast* (1987). These lively films, both shot on 16mm colour film, used the genre to draw a map of unemployment in Britain, and outlined very different political and emotional routes or reactions in response to the social deprivation of the era. *Fords* and *Coast* were both funded to contrasting degrees by television: *Fords* was a British Film Institute (BFI) Production Board project which received some completion funding from Channel 4, and the BBC was the majority funder of *Coast*. Neither film to date has been made available on VHS or DVD and, despite their television sponsorship, neither film has been re-broadcast since the year of their original transmission.

These factors have, of course, contributed to their obscurity, although *Coast* has a sizeable cult following on Internet forums, partly sustained by the availability of an off-air VHS recording via YouTube. Both comedies have a central inter-racial friendship at their heart and each has a vibrant soundtrack, featuring respectively a Keith Donald jazz saxophone score (*Fords*) and Motown soul classics (*Coast*). They take the problem and reality of unemployment as their point of departure and feature the cream of British character actors from the period (Pete Postlethwaite appearing in both films). However, the two films could not be more different in key aspects of tone, humour, politics and aesthetics. In the case of *Fords*, a textual analysis and production history will be combined with a study of this unusual and somewhat problematic film's critical reception. This will give a sense of how the film – both as text and project – reflected the fraught political climate of the Thatcherite 1980s and the turbulent changes which the British film industry was undergoing. With regard to the more conventional *Coast*, which will function as a complementary example, the emphasis will be predominantly on the production history, but with particular attention paid to the difficulties involved for those pursuing theatrical release for the Corporation's films at this time.

Rather than merely dwelling on 'roadblocks' or missed opportunities, the article will examine a number of contextual aspects that help us make sense of these 'lost boys': the importance of the TV funding of feature films in what was an increasingly costly film-making climate; the shifting strategic priorities of both the BFI and the BBC during a pivotal moment in the history of their film-making activities; and the issues and difficulties involved in finding the right balance between social or political critique and comedy and generic conventions.

The 'bi-racial buddy movie' and road movie genres (both films fit both of these categories) have been developed with huge success in the United States but have been largely untried in the United Kingdom. These hybridised films, made by young film-makers, subsisted only at the very low-budget level, and had very brief screen lives, as we will see. In this way *Fords* and *Coast* also seem to map out several roads not taken in British film culture during the intervening years, and pose the question of why these were dead ends.

Fords on Water: *politics and aesthetics*

To begin considering these issues, we must firstly outline the narrative of *Fords on Water*, which will give us an insight into the film's political outlook on Thatcher's Britain. *Fords* is the story of Winston (Elvis Payne) and Eddie (Mark Wingett), two young and innocent 'dole-survivors' (black and white, respectively) who meet through multiple coincidences and decide to take a road trip in Winston's Ford Escort to the North East of England to escape from their predicaments. Winston has just been made redundant, and finds that his fiancée's father now sees him as a threat to his family's bourgeois existence – hence he has failed to make it in white society. Eddie is a working-class lad who just wants to settle down but has been dumped by his girlfriend, to whom he had very recently proposed.

Winston and Eddie first meet in the taut opening scene when Winston is violently assaulted by a group of white youths due to the colour of his skin and Eddie manages to scare off the group after he tries and fails to hail a passing police car. As Barbara Lehin has noted, although *Fords* – along with other contemporary British films such as *Babylon* (1980), *Made in Britain* (1983) and *My Beautiful Laundrette* (1985) – features a cross-race friendship, 'racism occupies a predominant position in what is presented as a fragmented British society' (2003: 180).

While on the road, Winston and Eddie – on a whim – hold up a post office in a Northern provincial town and pick up a hitch-hiker, Beryl, who is an underground political activist with whom Eddie becomes infatuated. Winston and Eddie's new friendship, however, quickly deteriorates. Eddie frets about the robbery and the sorry state of his love life, while Winston becomes increasingly aloof and paranoid due to worries about the brother and father he has left behind – trade union activists who are being spied on by the police at the Ford car factory where they work. The paranoia of Winston (who carries a gun) grows as the two young men frequently encounter military convoys and roadblocks. After their return to London, however, the film ends on a positive note, with Winston's smile to the camera, after it becomes clear that Winston, who appears increasingly unstable and suicidal, has in fact faked his own death in order to elude the police. The film was described in the 1983 *London Film Festival Programme* as playing 'on the distinction between escapism and optimism', and it is suffused with anarchic energy, bitter humour, and a socialist outlook on the state of the nation. This rather volatile combination proved too much for some. Thus Mark Le Fanu observed:

> You feel almost that a decision has been made among the comrades that comedy will be the best way of 'putting the message across'. True and popular comedy depends on a broader consensus than this film is able to muster. The anger of the filmmaker's position keeps on peeping out from behind its 'disguise' to freeze the fun before it gets going. But maybe the director's anger isn't your anger or my anger in the first place. (1984: 17)

But while Le Fanu had a point about the 'freezing' of the humour, the review seems disproportionately preoccupied by what it regards as the incompatibility of the film's left-wing politics with humour, and insists that the troubles in Northern Ireland are 'not such a suitable subject for comedy', taking the film to task by recounting alleged IRA crimes of the period. This interpretation of the film's political themes, however, depends heavily on a quote from the film's publicity which apparently referred to the way in which the film shows 'everyday Ulster reality in mainland Britain' (ibid.). A recent interview with the director Barry Bliss[1] confirmed that he had had no involvement in this publicity copy, and no reference to Northern Ireland featured within either the film or any of the original drafts of the script.

Clearly this was not intended to be the subject of the film – it was at most a subtext. In a sense the film had been overtaken by the kind of events which echoed the breakdown in social order which the film portrayed, and this served to determine the polarised reception it received. As Julian Petley noted in a contemporary review, the vision of Britain in *Fords* 'looks frighteningly like Northern Ireland, with its constant roadblocks and massive military and police presence' (1984: 150). In his view, the scenes of Britain's roads being closed to the public for reasons of 'security' seemed 'ominously prescient' at the time of the film's theatrical release, given recent events at Greenham Common and the Nottinghamshire coalfields (ibid.). In addition, although it was referred to as 'a deft piece of political future shock' (Adair and Roddick 1985: 84), the idea was to create a scenario perilously close to present reality. Therefore it can instead be regarded as a counterfactual film: 'If it's happening there (in Ulster), why can't it happen here?'[2] Iain Johnstone in *The Sunday Times*, 29 April 1984, described the world of the film as a 'Britain of the near future which [Bliss] envisages as having 5m unemployed and insufficient welfare to feed them in a semi-police state which has outlawed unofficial strikes. A bleak, hopefully fanciful vision but decidedly more possible than that of Orwell.'

All this raises the issue of the topicality of the TV play or TV movie versus the full-blooded feature film, a subject which was widely debated at that time. Compared to plays, films – and especially co-productions – typically had lengthier production schedules and were subject to theatrical windows before being shown on television. According to Francke and Wrathall, this meant that 'instead of the immediacy of a *Play for Today* there is a more generalised statement tailored for a potentially wider audience' (1987: 58). Or, as Mamoun Hassan stated: 'Television films and programmes have to be topical; cinema films have to be more universal than timely' (quoted in Houston et al. 1984: 116). The TV critic Sean Day-Lewis also reflected this sentiment in the *Guardian*, 17 August 1987, complaining about the way in which TV viewers were often 'short-changed' by 'an excessive tilt to the cinema': 'A good film may still be a good film three years later. It is just as likely to be tuned to its time and to contain a built-in obsolescence that will soon show.'

The example of *Fords on Water* demonstrates, however, that some-times a film could indeed be timely and prescient despite – or because of – the delays incurred by lengthy pre-production and theatrical release phases. It also demonstrates the fact that publicity materials and theatrical exhibition can offer an opportunity to inflect a film with a more specific and topical political resonance, with or without the permission of the film-maker. One of Bliss's actual intentions was to adopt an energetic and working-class perspective rather than make a film suffused with middle-class guilt. As John Akomfrah observed, for Bliss, the film was made 'in part to combat views of the working class in defeat and decline. It is not a film racked with the guilt and introspection characteristic of current political drama' – and he cites *The Ploughman's Lunch* as an example of the latter (1984: 16).

Fords on Water provides an insight into the exigencies and dif-ficulties of political film-making at the time – the attempt by the self-proclaimed 'only Trotskyist filmmaker around' (quoted in ibid.) to make his first intervention in the feature film arena – and also the ways in which the intended message was diluted, distorted or rejected. The original script for *Fords on Water* included more explicit political

imagery that was removed or obscured in the final film. One sequence
is described as follows:

> We now pass through a village with people sitting around, doing nothing.
> They have no work. They look bored and frustrated. Then we see a series
> of small towns etc., with shops and factories closed, picket lines trying
> to save jobs, demonstrations, occupations of factories and businesses,
> confrontations with the police. We see fighting in the streets, between the
> police and workers, and worker against worker. (Bliss and Colvill n.d.: 23)

It will be instructive at this point to examine the film's development
history and the reasons behind these script modifications. On the
strength of two shorts which he made with funding from the Greater
London Arts Association in the late 1970s – *You Winning?* (1978) and
Sandbags and Trenches (1979) – and largely due to this work being championed by film-maker Maurice Hatton (then on the BFI Production
Board), Barry Bliss was approached by the BFI in 1980 with the offer
of script development funding for a potential feature film project.
A condition of the offer was that he would work with an already
established co-writer – Billy Colvill – who was perfectly acceptable to
Bliss because he already knew him. Colvill was a playwright and
actor whose work was often produced at the Half Moon Theatre in
Stepney, and he had recently acted in Stephen Frears' *Bloody Kids*
(1979), a spirited attack on Thatcher's Britain. Both Colvill and Bliss
were young men from working-class backgrounds, which was rare in
the independent film sector, and this also helped them to bond with
Peter Sainsbury, then head of the BFI Production Board, who was of a
broadly similar background and generation.[3]

Although the project therefore had an auspicious start, this was not
set to continue. Upon submission in 1981, the script was rejected – an
unexpected outcome for Bliss and Colvill, especially as it had been
solicited by the Production Board in the first place. They were, however, offered a reprieve of sorts with the opportunity of resubmitting
the following year. In the meantime the television playwright Howard
Schuman came on board as script advisor, together with the industry
veteran Verity Lambert as (uncredited) executive producer. Schuman
had recently been appointed to the Production Board by Lambert,
who had become its chair in July 1981. Schuman encouraged Bliss and
Colvill to tone down the politics of the project, moving it away from
agit-prop towards a (slightly) more conventional road movie, although
he recently admitted that in retrospect he had felt too 'emotionally
close' to the project to be able to offer the critical support needed to
get the script 'into shape':

> My abiding memory of this process was that I liked Barry and Billy tremendously and was at one with the radical political ideas and what they were trying to achieve technically – marrying radical politics with a jazzy/poppy style ... However, because I liked them so much personally, I wasn't strong enough/critical enough to help them improve the script.[4]

Presented again to the BFI, the revised script was accepted (although the vote in favour was by the narrowest of margins) in July 1982. Allegedly, however, just days before principal shooting was due to commence, Lambert insisted on major script revisions. Schuman played a crucial role in brokering a compromise which mitigated the most drastic of revisions, but Bliss nonetheless had essentially to rewrite the script over the course of a weekend.

This was arguably a conflation of editorial advice and control, and possibly, therefore, an infringement of the film-maker's rights. The Production Board's policy in this respect was described in March 1983 as follows: 'Whereas the Production Board has no editorial control over a script once selected suggestions can [*sic*] be made, the individual members of the Board seek to be accessible to help and advise film-makers' (Beecham and Walsh 1983: 9). Colin MacCabe, who was appointed to the Production Board at the same time as Schuman, was later to take the view that the Board should 'give the director all the "aggro and hard input" associated with a commercial producer with the difference that ultimately the director always has the final say' (quoted in Petrie 1990: 189).

However such professional ethics are viewed, this arguably had a limited effect in defusing the political anger of the film's script, which still delineated a landscape of unemployment, snobbery, racial tension and industrial unrest. Unfortunately, what it undoubtedly did was damage the coherence of the film. As the *Variety* review for the film noted:

> Newcomer Barry Bliss, helming his first feature, shows directorial promise: his handling is imaginative and inventive. He's hampered, however, by a muddled script, written by himself and Billy Colvill, which seems to strive for cynical comedy as well as a bleak view of a Britain filled with unemployed workers, growing militancy, and a smothering military presence; the narrative is aimless and the humour is thin on the ground. (Anon. 1989: 211)

Bliss and Colvill had clearly intended the film to have a loose and non-linear narrative featuring multiple flashback and dream sequences from the perspective of both Winston and Eddie, but the hasty processes of rewriting and editing the film meant a further reshuffling of scenes. Fortunately the loose and episodic nature of the road movie provided just enough latitude, while Jean-Luc Godard's prototypical road movies provided inspiration and a precedent for how a freewheeling approach can help to navigate obstacles and accidents.

More specifically, the influence of Godard can be detected in the aesthetics, surrealism and self-reflexivity of particular scenes. In particular, there is Eddie's dream sequence about Beryl, the underground political activist and new object of his affections. Seemingly as a response to Eddie's question (in voice-over): 'What's it like where you live?' there is a cut to Beryl standing on a hill, making a soap-box speech (to camera) about the despoiling of her area ('They tried to take our livelihood ... we won't let them!') as a huge cooling tower is demolished behind her, which is a remarkable screen spectacle. There is then a cut to a tracking shot of Beryl and Eddie marching down a terraced street, triumphantly leading a group of children and young people in a procession – this is Eddie's dream of 'participating in an impressive display of popular strength' (Petley 1984: 150). As the camera cranes up past a power-line and over the rooftops of the terrace, it mingles with the smoke from the chimneys and we hear the saxophone strains of Keith Donald's jazz score.

The effect is exhilarating but is quickly undercut with a jarring edit as we return to earth with a bump in the form of the dingy pub bedroom in which Eddie wakes up alone, Beryl having departed without him. But as Petley has observed, this oblique approach had its drawbacks:

> The emotive power of the images rather depends on the spectator already knowing that Beryl's home is in fact Chopwell, known as Little Moscow or Little Russia on account of its sustained resistance in the General Strike, and that the cooling tower which collapses so startlingly behind her back as she looks towards the camera marks the virtual destruction of the one-time steel town of nearby Consett. (1984: 150)

Here the surrealism of the film erases the traces of its local or regional specificity and thereby some of the acuteness and topicality of its political attack, hence John Akomfrah's rather more vague commentary in *City Limits* about 'visible signs of structural collapse and decomposition', such as 'giant foundries simply crumbling in full view' in a 'brilliantly alien Britain' (1984: 16). As well as Godard, such scenes are reminiscent of the popular surrealism of Richard Lester and are key to the film's departure from the norms and conventions of social realism. As Sheila Johnston noted in a review for *Time Out*: 'With its lustrous, colourful images and laconic screenplay, its jump cuts and jazzy score, it owes less to drab naturalism than to the moody poetry of Neil Jordan's *Angel*, spiked with Nouvelle Vague verve and nerve' (quoted in Milne and Pym 2007: 405).

As can be seen in the imaginative camerawork, art direction and cinematography of *Fords*, Bliss had been keen to depart from naturalism, especially as he had already adopted a more conventional social realist approach in *You Winning?*: 'I didn't want to be Ken Loach or Les Blair – I wanted to create a different form of cinema'.[5] As well as Godard's surrealism and harsh colourisation, Bliss has cited the dreamlike imagery which pervaded some of the work of Italian directors Bertolucci, Antonioni and Rosi and of cinematographer Vittorio Storaro as key influences. *Fords* was a brave attempt to extend the domain of realism from the objective world of British naturalism to 'the subjective domain: the psychic realism of Antonioni and Bergman', to use Duncan Petrie's formulation about the distinctions between British and European approaches to cinema (1990: 289). In doing so Bliss pursued an impulse to experiment and bridge worlds by presenting 'hard politics within a poetic showcase'.[6]

Industry context: the BFI Production Board

Although departing from them radically in style and temperament, what *Fords* shared with other movies part-funded by television at the time, such as *Looks and Smiles* (1982), *Meantime* (1983), *Letter to Brezhnev* (1985) and *Vroom* (1988), was the way in which it sought to highlight unemployment and give roles to the unemployed (Lehin 2003: 72). Such films denounced the actions of the Thatcher government – sometimes, ironically, with the help of public money. Indeed Bliss was accused by an audience member at the London Film Festival screening of *Fords* of biting the hand that fed him. Despite the importance of television funding, the burgeoning of low-budget realist films dealing with contemporary issues during this period was not simply a result of a strong generic tradition that had been fostered by British television. The government's dismantling in 1985 of subsidy structures such as the Eady Levy and the restricted budgets of the BFI and the National Film Finance Corporation (NFFC) also largely explained the trend towards the production of low-budget films. It can be argued that these industrial factors, combined with the predilection on the part of commissioners like Mamoun Hassan (Managing Director of the NFFC) and David Rose (Commissioning

Editor for Fiction at Channel 4) for social and poetic realism and films grounded in contemporary reality, had an impact on the content of the scripts submitted (Lehin 2003: 42–4).

During the period in which *Fords* was commissioned, the BFI Production Board was in the process of transforming its policies away from a dogmatic approach to awarding only the 'correct mix' of politics and aesthetic experiment. Under the chairmanship of Verity Lambert, it instead partly aimed to provide a bridge for young directors between the grants offered by Regional Arts Associations and the commercial mainstream of the industry. Much of the training role of the Production Board had been taken over by film schools (*Coast to Coast* director Sandy Johnson was a graduate of the National Film and Television School), but it still felt a responsibility to take on relatively inexperienced film-makers. This may help to explain Lambert's last-minute anxieties about the film's script; perhaps she was anxious that the politics of *Fords* should not hinder the film's prospects and, by extension, the Board's strategy. More attention was also being devoted to art-house distribution and exhibition: *The Draughtsman's Contract* (1982) had a hugely successful run at the Screen on the Hill while *Fords on Water* had a much shorter run (29 April to 10 May 1984) at the Ritzy Cinema in Brixton.

Although very different from one another, these two films exemplified what might be described as a 'mid-range' BFI Production Board project from the period: neither a short film or documentary intended to provide post-film school experience (up to £100,000 budget), nor a larger-budgeted project helmed by a film-maker with prior Production Board experience (for example a £500,000 budget). In a Production Division report dated 10 October 1983, Peter Sainsbury described this production category and its precarious status as follows:

> Second production category: Films costing up to £300,000 normally low budget feature films heavily dependent upon concessionary agreements with Trade Unions, financed by the Institute using its OAL [Office of Arts and Libraries] grant and subventions from other organizations and far more modest productions than many that have been undertaken recently: professional standards will be maintained but crews will be as small as possible, casts very small, locations few and close at hand and subjects contemporary. In this category the central concerns of the production policy are expressed addressing itself to experiment on one hand and to media and audiences on the other, but the activity will be heavily curtailed by the rise in costs and fall in available resources that have made productions like 'The Draughtsman's Contract' (1981) or 'Fords on Water' (1982) impossible today. (1983: 2)

Sainsbury's stark assessment and prediction here seem quite startling, given the neoteric status of these films. At the time, the BFI's low-budget feature programme was anticipated to be a trend that could 'continue with less need of Channel 4's help' (Willmott 1983: 17) and the fruitful partnership between the BFI and Channel 4 that was inaugurated by *The Draughtsman's Contract* is typically thought to mark a golden era in the history of the Production Board. Yet it is significant that, at least before the New Directors scheme of the early 1990s, this partnership benefitted already-proven auteurs such as Peter Greenaway, Derek Jarman, Bill Douglas and Terence Davies, who had relatively larger budgets at their disposal, rather than young first-time film-makers like Bliss.

Despite its modest scope, the mid-range category or strategy described above quickly became a victim of economic and ideological pressures on the Board and highly dependent on completion money from Channel 4, in addition to the channel's annual subvention of £500,000 to the BFI. *Fords on Water* was partly funded by Alan Fountain's Independent Film and Video Department and was screened on the Department's *Eleventh Hour* slot on 27 May 1985. Fountain did not have a budget specifically allocated to feature films, but did manage to 'support [British] film-makers working in a much more European tradition' than the typically more established film-makers supported by Rose's Film on Four (Fountain, quoted in Petrie 1990: 167). However, Fountain's budget was almost entirely tied up with the regional film and video workshops that it funded, the majority of which were geared more toward producing documentary material than feature films. It is a measure of the interdependent nature of these limited subsidies that, within a couple of years, there would be resentment within the BFI that its own commitment to the workshops was such that the Production Board could afford to fund only one or two feature-length productions per year (Auty 1985: 69).

The BFI's dependence on Channel 4 as a partner was evident as early as 1983, when Channel 4 provided 55 per cent of the Board's production monies. At this time, it was expected that this would increase due to rising costs (particularly of the BFI/ACTT/Channel 4 Code of Practice), the reduction of the amount of money that the BFI itself could put into the production pot and 'the punitive attitude that Equity [the actors union] has – after three years of negotiation – finally taken to the transmission of BFI films by the Channel ... [which] has been such as [to] turn the 1981/82 Channel Four subvention into more of a loan than a grant' (Sainsbury 1983: 3). The increasing reliance on television funding in British film culture was impossible to ignore. As Penelope Houston observed of the event in which *Fords on Water* received its (official) premiere: 'The 1983 London Film Festival included a hefty line-up of new British productions. It would have been a pathetic entry if it had been restricted to films made for cinemas' (1984: 115).

Coast to Coast: *the journey from script to small screen*

The role of television in funding feature films was to become even more crucial in the years that followed. With this in mind, we can now turn our attention to *Coast to Coast*, which received almost all of its funding from the BBC and was broadcast in the *Screen Two* strand in 1987. As noted earlier, *Fords* was a social drama only in as much as it sought to examine issues such as unemployment, racial prejudice and state repression; in utilising a dynamic visual style, radical politics and surreal comedy it sought to deviate from the social realist tradition. *Coast to Coast* had no such political or aesthetic ideals or ambitions; it was a straightforward comedy caper about two men, an unemployed black DJ (Ritchie, played by Lenny Henry) and a deserter from the US army (John Carloff, played by John Shea), drawn together by their love of soul music. Ritchie and Carloff decide to avoid the monotony of existence on the dole in Liverpool by hitting the road with a mobile disco, but are soon on the run from both gangsters and the police.

Inspired by screenwriter Stan Hey's experiences of frequenting black nightclubs in Liverpool as a teenager (an early scene features John Carloff's flashback of attending The Sink Club in Liverpool), the film was a love letter to soul music. However, it was also peopled by small-time crooks and loafers – brilliantly portrayed by British character actors such as Pete Postlethwaite and Peter Vaughan. *Coast* was unashamedly parochial in its humour and references, and embraced the ironies inherent in being an English road movie. In this respect it was very different from *Fords*, which instead had a certain 'un-British quality' in recalling the 'iconoclastic spirit of the Nouvelle Vague' (Petley 1984: 150).

Although the BBC was unanimously perceived to be lagging behind Channel 4's example when it came to the funding of feature films at this time, the Corporation was arguably just as – if not more – flexible when it came to genre. It is notable that a *City Limits* article from 1987 commended *Coast to Coast* (albeit described as a 'quasi-road movie') for 'extending the range of TV drama' (Francke and Wrathall 1987: 58). What the article did find lacking about the *Screen Two* series in which it appeared, however, was 'the interest in contemporary social and political issues that [had] distinguished the '60s and early '70s TV play'. Peter Goodchild (then Head of Plays and Drama at the BBC) conceded that 'the latest batch are less issue-orientated: they're not like *Spongers* or *United Kingdom*' (cited in ibid.). Thus while *Fords* received criticism for being too political, *Coast* received criticism for not being political enough.

Sandy Johnson, who directed *Coast to Coast*, has recently suggested that the political dimension of the film was embodied in Ritchie's decision to hit the road, knowing that he didn't have any other options given the dearth of jobs: 'I don't think Stan wanted to make that [unemployment] an issue. We were aware that the opportunities for him were limited – music was a way of escaping from that'.[7] The character of John Carloff also sought escape – from the US Army and the expectations of his top-brass military father – which was a theme which was to be explored in the planned sequel, called *Brother to Brother*.

After Johnson had read the script for *Coast to Coast*, which had been delivered to him by Hey, he immediately set about trying to source funds to realise the project as a feature film. The two men initially brought in Brian Eastman as a producer and cast the boxer John Conteh as Ritchie, but failed to find funding. On a whim, Johnson sent the script to the BBC but heard nothing back until much later, when he received a phone call from the BBC drama producer Graham Benson who said that he loved the script and asked Johnson if he could start work on the project immediately:

> What had actually happened was another *Screen Two* drama had been cancelled for reasons I didn't know, but in those days, you had to fit slots for your project, and your producers at the BBC. So Graham Benson had a crew and services, and the whole set-up to make a film, with dates, with everyone committed, but he had no script. Literally they'd gone back to find a script they thought that they would also like to make, and that's why I got started so quickly.[8]

After the project had been given the green light, Johnson had some new ideas, including casting Lenny Henry as the lead character Ritchie, which was to be the comedian's first acting role. John Shea was cast as the American John Carloff after Jeff Bridges – the first choice for the role – had written to say that he loved the script but was not able to commit to the shooting schedule. In sharp contrast to the long pre-production and tortuous editorial negotiations to which *Fords* was subject, *Coast* was fast-tracked into production. It was shot on 16mm in five weeks (between 17 February and 21 March 1986), and was broadcast as the first film of the third series of *Screen Two* on 4 January 1987.

Coast to Coast was widely acclaimed and, combined with other successes from the same series such as *Northanger Abbey*, *Will You Love Me Tomorrow*, *Naming the Names* and *Inappropriate Behaviour*, its shortage of visual delights could be overlooked, as the series was collectively regarded as evidence that the BBC was 'as capable of turning out cinema quality products as any of its rivals' (Thomas 1987: 23). It was promptly repeated on BBC1, in a prestigious slot at Easter. However, the film never received a theatrical release beyond a handful of screenings at festivals in Europe and America after it had been transmitted on television.

This was some years before the BBC had established their stand-alone film arm, BBC Films, and at the time none of the BBC's *Screen Two* productions received any sort of theatrical release, largely due to the relationship between the Corporation and the craft unions. The BBC did not recognise the ACTT union, whose members received higher rates of pay than the BBC technician's union BETA, and BETA was refusing to countenance the theatrical release of films made with its members. The film's executive producer, David Nicholas Wilkinson, who had been the first independent producer to work with the Corporation on film projects (with Colin Gregg's *From the Lighthouse* in 1983), received an extremely attractive offer for *Coast* from a US distributor, but this initiative was apparently blocked by Michael Grade (then the BBC's Director of Programmes), as it would have meant 'setting a precedent'.[9] A similar precedent soon was set, however, when, after months of negotiations, a one-off BETA agreement allowed *Little Sweetheart* (aka *Poison Candy* and *Little Sister*, 1989), a co-production between the BBC and Anthony Simmons' independent production company West One, to receive a limited theatrical release outside the UK.

Addressing the Independent Programme Producers Association (IPPA) conference on 31 March 1987, the newly appointed BBC Director General Michael Checkland announced that independents would be able to acquire theatrical rights for projects commissioned by the BBC, provided that the films were made entirely outside of the BBC's production facilities (Harbord 1987: 3). This was some years before the imposition of both the BBC's 'internal market' policy known as 'Producer Choice' and the 25 per cent quota for the commissioning of independent productions, but Checkland had adopted what he termed an 'open arms' policy towards independents. All this brought the Corporation a step closer towards parity with the model of Channel 4's Film on Four, whose success had forced the Corporation to re-examine its attitudes towards making films (rather than plays), and which in many ways had been the inspiration behind their *Screen Two* strand.

In 1988 Martyn Auty commissioned Sandy Johnson and Stan Hey to go to the US on a 'recce' for a planned sequel to *Coast to Coast*, to be set and filmed in the States, which was to be called *Brother to Brother*. While this trip was successful and Hey wrote a script, the project failed to find outside funding to top up its budget and was therefore regarded as too expensive.[10]

At this time it was becoming clear to the BBC that it needed theatrical release for financial reasons, as well as to increase its profile. As Peter Goodchild admitted candidly at the time: 'The licence funding scheme puts a definite roof on what we are able to achieve. Our main hope of increasing our revenue is the possibility of theatrical release' (quoted in Smith 1988: 15). A major reason for Mark Shivas' appointment that year as Head of Drama at the BBC was his experience in film, and his commitment to the view, expressed in the *Observer*, 24 September 1989, that 'a cinema release in advance of a television showing gives publicity to a movie and a lifespan denied to a TV film'. Before it was bolstered by the arrival of Shivas, the BBC lacked financial clout, opportunities for theatrical release and expertise in attaining co-production finance.

Although *Coast* had all the ingredients of a commercial success, it was thus denied the possibility of theatrical release, but there were other factors which precluded the film from achieving success in the longer term. Firstly, Wilkinson had set up a number of overseas sales, but these fell through after several partners in the London-based distribution company he had used to establish these sales were found to have embezzled funds; as a result his investors never even received all their money back.[11] Without a theatrical release, and without these overseas sales, the film's hopes of ever fully recouping its costs were dashed.

Secondly, Sandy Johnson and Stan Hey were adamant that the film had to feature a soundtrack of Tamla Motown classics, especially as specific songs had been chosen to accompany key scenes, with song titles and lyrics mirroring predicaments faced by characters. Although Johnson achieved something of a coup by getting the rights-holders of Tamla Motown to agree to this heavy usage of their material, this was solely restricted to two television transmissions. Wilkinson has recently recalled that an agreement with the label Stax Records would have also allowed for VHS release.[12]

Finally, the film was made under a standard BBC rights and contracts agreement which stipulated that all those involved in making the film were contracted only for a fourteen-year term, which has long since expired. This, on top of the expense of the music licensing rights, means it is very unlikely that the film will be ever be re-transmitted or released. This is most unfortunate, as *Coast to Coast* has clearly generated a minor cult following, unlike *Fords on Water* which languishes in obscurity.

In considering the reasons for this, we must remember that *Fords* was an edgy and experimental feature film helmed by a first-time film-maker whereas *Coast* director Sandy Johnson was tried and tested, with experience directing feature-length TV comedy in the shape of several of Channel 4's *Comic Strip Presents . . .* films. As previously noted, *Coast* also featured the acting debut of a much-loved British comedian, a screenplay that featured some unforgettable gags and throwaway lines, and an unremittingly upbeat soundtrack. With the benefit of hindsight the edginess and uneven humour of the cinematic *Fords* could not compete with the effortless vernacular and TV pedigree of *Coast* and be sustained in the collective memory of viewers.

Conclusion

While US cinema has recognised the profitability of both buddy-road movies and bi-racial buddy movies, these sub-genres have been practically non-existent in Britain, and rare examples have been oriented toward comedy rather than action. This aspect of the cultural divide was the source of much of the humour of British action comedy *Hot Fuzz* (2007)—a buddy movie in which the main characters are young policemen who escape the monotony and tiny scale of English provincial village life by studying and aping action moves from *Point Break* (1991) and *Bad Boys 2* (2003). In general the disparity between the UK and US contexts also reminds us of the often-commented incongruity or absurdity of the very idea of an English road movie. This is a constant feature of Ritchie and Carloff's zigzag course across England (from Liverpool to Harwich via the Lake District) in *Coast*, much of which takes place in an ice-cream van kitted out as a mobile disco.

The particular nature of the humour of *Coast* meant that the film was consistently characterised by its lack of glamour, which was partly determined and reinforced by its TV movie status. While budget constraints contributed to the charm and inventiveness of the film, they also contributed to the lack of exposure which it received in an increasingly competitive marketplace. David Wilkinson (the executive producer on *Coast*) believes that it is exemplary of the dangers of trying to copy an American genre with a limited budget,[13] as US distributors are more interested in films that portray a quirky or period version or vision of British culture and heritage.

Both films undoubtedly adopted the road movie genre partly for pragmatic reasons: as a means to allow for an assessment of the 'condition of England' (in the radical tradition of William Cobbett) in the case of *Fords*, or to adopt a more conventional (and American) on-the-run escape narrative in the case of *Coast*. But as a genre its open road or 'tabula rasa' simplicity has often been deceptive; David Laderman believes it is defined by its 'repeated positioning of conservative values and rebellious desires in an uncomfortable, often depoliticized dialectic' (quoted in Cohan and Hark 2002: 3). It was rare indeed for a road movie to be as politicised as *Fords* – and especially one that also incorporated comedy. *Fords* moved beyond what Laderman has termed the 'visionary rebellion' of the countercultural road movie (2010), and, while it retained something of a post-punk attitude, it did not subscribe to the postmodernism and nihilism that would characterise certain road movies of the new era. *Coast*, with its nostalgia for 1960s soul music, was far less ambivalent about its subcultural influences and allegiances.

It almost goes without saying that, as bi-racial buddy-road movies, the films were characterised by diversity but not by gender equality. However, while John Akomfrah (1984: 16) noted of *Fords* that 'Winston and Eddie's relationship is secured by identifying the women in their lives as part of "the problem"', it is certainly the case that Beryl challenges Eddie's and Winston's aimlessness and facade of bravado; Bliss has stated 'the thing our critics never understood was that Beryl was the hero and political heart of the film'.[14] Women are largely peripheral to the narrative of *Coast*. Like the British TV comedy staple *Auf Wiedersehen, Pet* (Stan Hey had written several episodes of the second series in 1984), it revolved around male camaraderie and 'wheeling and dealing' (Holland 2013: 122).

The two films also provide an interesting 'yin and yang' comparison in other ways. *Fords* represented a missed opportunity to achieve what Peter Stead ultimately found lacking in the films of the 1980s – the use of comedy to reach both young audiences and wider audiences in the service of social critique. As he concluded at the end of the decade:

> Film comedies in Britain still seem to pull their punches a little and it is almost as if the industry has deliberately refrained from making a totally challenging and anarchic social comment in *The Boys from the Black Stuff* vein ... The writer Hanif Kureishi is on record as suggesting that in

the Britain of the 1980s 'everything is so horrific' that people are no longer interested in social realism but the whole point about comedy, as he was well aware, is that it can achieve a cutting edge denied straight documentary even as it appeals to mass audiences. (1989: 217)

While the 'future-shocked' *Fords* contained social comment but under-performed as a comedy, *Coast* performed assuredly as a comedy but refrained from social comment in favour of nostalgic impulses. *Fords* had a short theatrical release which was denied to *Coast*, and while its commercial prospects were far more limited, it did achieve far more aesthetically to earn the outing away from the small screen.

What both films shared, apart from the remarkable similarities in their basic premise and their liveliness, sharpness and fast pace, was the fleeting nature of their screen lives. Inevitably, therefore, this is something of a story of missed opportunities. Ironically, Channel 4 experienced critical and commercial success shortly after *Fords* was broadcast on television with films that were characterised by a relatively high quotient of anarchic humour and social comment, such as *My Beautiful Laundrette* (1985) and *Letter to Brezhnev* (1985). Although *Coast* experienced success in the UK TV context, there was no coordinated strategy to give it further exposure, and the planned sequel never materialised. Perhaps from the foregoing discussion we can deduce various reasons why both prototypes of the British bi-racial buddy-road movie failed to make the running.

Acknowledgements
Many thanks to Barry Bliss, Sandy Johnson, Howard Schuman and David Wilkinson for giving their time to be interviewed and/or respond to queries, and to Rosie Gleeson, Information & Archives Manager at Channel 4, for kindly providing some useful press cuttings.

Notes
1. Barry Bliss, interview with the author, 3 April 2014.
2. Ibid.
3. Ibid.
4. Howard Schuman, personal communication with the author, 21 April 2014.
5. Bliss interview.
6. Ibid.
7. Sandy Johnson, interview with the author, 19 April 2014.
8. Ibid.
9. David Wilkinson, interview with the author, 12 May 2014.
10. Johnson interview.
11. Wilkinson interview.
12. Ibid.
13. Ibid.
14. Bliss interview.

References

Adair, G. and Roddick, N. (1985), *A Night at the Pictures: Ten Decades of British Film*, London: Columbus Books.

Akomfrah, J. (1984), 'Walking on water', *City Limits*, 27 May, p. 16.

Anon. (1989), *Variety Film Reviews 1983–1984*, New Providence, NJ: R. R. Bowker.

Auty, M. (1985), 'But is it cinema?', in M. Auty and N. Roddick (eds), *British Cinema Now*, London: British Film Institute, pp. 57–70.

Beecham, S. and Walsh, M. (1983), 'Behind the BFI no. 5: The Production Division', *Film*, 114, March, pp. 8–9.

Bliss, B. and Colvill, B. (n.d.), 'Fords on Water Annotated Script', SCR 10251, British Film Institute Special Collections.

Cohan, S. and Hark, I. R. (2002), 'Introduction', in S. Cohan and I. R. Hark (eds), *The Road Movie Book*, London: Routledge, pp. 1–16.

Francke, L. and Wrathall, J. (1987), 'Network news TV & film special', *City Limits*, 2 April, p. 58

Harbord, J. (1987), 'Hope rises over BBC cinema deal', *Broadcast*, 16 April, p. 3.

Holland, P. (2013), *Broadcasting and the NHS in the Thatcherite 1980s: The Challenge to Public Service*, London: Palgrave Macmillan.

Houston, P. (ed.) with Hassan, M., Puttnam, D., Isaacs, J., Perry, S., Millar, G., Bennett, A. and Parker, A. (1984), 'British cinema: life before death on television?', *Sight and Sound*, 53: 2, Spring, pp. 115–22.

Laderman, D. (2010), *Driving Visions: Exploring the Road Movie*, Austin, TX: University of Texas Press.

Le Fanu, M. (1984), '*Fords on Water*', *Films and Filming*, July, p. 17.

Lehin, B. (2003), *Cinema and Society: Thatcher's Britain and Mitterand's France*, PhD thesis, University of Warwick. Available at < http://webcat.warwick.ac.uk/record=b1735807~S15 > (accessed 3 March 2014).

Milne, T. and Pym, J. (2007), *Time Out Film Guide*. London: Penguin Books.

Petley, J. (1984), '*Fords on Water*', *Monthly Film Bulletin*, May, pp. 149–50.

Petrie, D. (1990), *Making Movies: The Structuring of Creativity in Contemporary British Cinema*, PhD thesis, University of Edinburgh. Available at < https://www.era.lib.ed.ac.uk/bitstream/1842/7376/1/293071.pdf > (accessed 8 April 2014).

Sainsbury, P. (1983), 'Current Opportunities and Problems in Film Production', unpublished BFI Production Board report, 18 October (Independent Film Video and Photography Association archive, Sheffield Hallam University).

Smith, J. U. (1988), 'The subtle symbiosis between television and film', *Broadcast*, 13 May, pp. 14–15.

Stead, P. (1989), *Film and the Working Class: The Feature Film in British and American Society*, London: Routledge, pp. 14–15.

Thomas, A. (1987), 'BBC moves closer to historic deal', *Television Today*, 2 April, p. 23.

Walker, J. (1985), *The Once and Future Film: British Cinema in the Seventies and Eighties*, London: Methuen.

Willmott, N. (1983), 'The saviour of the silver screen', *Broadcast*, 28 October, pp. 13–17.

Ieuan Franklin is Lecturer in Film and Media Theory at Bournemouth University and Wiltshire College (Salisbury). Between 2010 and 2014 he worked as Research Assistant on the AHRC-funded project 'Channel 4 and British Film Culture' project at the University of Portsmouth.

Assessing Cultural Impact: Film4, Canon Formation and Forgotten Films

Laura Mayne

Abstract:

For over 30 years Channel 4 has supported more than 400 feature films through its production arm, Film4. However, despite the scale and variety of this contribution to British cinema, only a handful of these productions are regularly cited in print media and academic texts as being representative of the Film4 catalogue and/or influential in British film culture generally. This article will look at the creation of top films lists as a case of canon formation, and the ways in which the Film4 canon in particular continues to be shaped and contested, not only by critics, academics and cultural institutions, but by Channel 4 itself. It draws upon the work of Janet Staiger (1985) on canon formation and of Joseph Lampel and Shivasharan Nadavulakere (2009) on retrospective consecration in order to consider the processes by which certain films are more likely to appear in critics' best films lists. Bearing in mind that the brand identity of Film4 depends also on Channel 4's own promotional activities, the article will go on to examine two case studies of Film4 anniversary seasons in order to assess the part that scheduling plays in constructing the channel's own representations of its contribution to British cinema. Finally, after exploring some of the reasons why certain films are remembered (and why others are forgotten), attention will turn to the ways in which certain forgotten films can be re-presented in DVD and video-on-demand markets. This reveals the extent to which commercial factors are also determinants in the processes of canon formation and can impinge upon the attribution of cultural value.

Keywords: canon formation; Channel 4; cultural impact; cultural value; Film4; retrospective consecration.

Journal of British Cinema and Television 11.4 (2014): 459–480
Edinburgh University Press
DOI: 10.3366/jbctv.2014.0229
© *Journal of British Cinema and Television*
www.euppublishing.com/jbctv

Laura Mayne

Introduction

Since 1982 Channel 4's film funding practices have changed the landscape of the British film industry, offered opportunities to emerging new talent, fostered innovative stylistic and aesthetic practices, and brought new images of Britain to cinema and television screens. Although the channel has supported over 400 features, only a handful of these productions are regularly cited in academic texts or by critics in their 'top films' lists as being influential in British cinema and/or the best examples of the Film4 catalogue.[1] Among the titles most regularly cited are *My Beautiful Laundrette* (1985), *Four Weddings and a Funeral* (1994), *Trainspotting* (1996) and *East is East* (1999). Through analysing the appearance of Channel 4 productions in various listings of top films, this article will explore the formation of the Film4 canon and will examine how this canon has been established, presented and contested by film critics in print media, by cultural institutions such as the British Film Institute (BFI) and by Channel 4 itself. At the most general level, it will enquire into the processes by which certain films gain cultural legitimisation and ask why this should be the case. More importantly, why are other films, which could also be deemed culturally influential, subsequently forgotten or overlooked in critical appraisals?

To guide this work, the article draws upon the work of Pierre Bourdieu and of Joseph Lampel and Shivasharan Nadavulakere on cultural consecration in order to argue that contemporaneous consecration (box-office popularity, awards and critical reception at the time of a film's release) can influence retrospective consecration by critics and institutions. Bearing in mind that the brand identity of Film4 depends also on Channel 4's own promotional activities, the article will go on to examine two case studies of Film4 anniversary seasons in order to assess the part that scheduling plays in constructing the channel's own representations of its contribution to British cinema. Finally, after exploring some of the reasons why certain films are remembered and why others are forgotten, attention will turn to the ways in which some forgotten films are re-presented in DVD and video-on-demand (VoD) markets. What the latter reveals is how commercial factors are also determinants in the processes of canon formation and can impinge upon the attribution of cultural value.

Measuring the impact and cultural value of British film

Over the past ten years, the cultural value of British film has received much attention, not least in research reports and studies of findings commissioned by institutions such as the now defunct UK Film Council (UKFC) and the BFI. The Narval Media et al. (2009) report *Stories We Tell Ourselves* and the Northern Alliance and Ipsos MediaCT (2011) report *Opening Our Eyes* were each followed by regional seminars held at UK universities, which promoted dialogues between academics, policy-makers and industry professionals. The methodology for *Stories We Tell Ourselves* involved drawing up a database of 5,000 films from 1946 to 2006. From this, a sample was taken of 200 random films and 200 films considered to have lasting impact (Narval Media et al. 2009). 'Impact' was measured in three ways: contemporaneous impact through the box office and awards, the afterlife of a film (DVD/video markets) and the wider impact (YouTube, IMDb, social influence). Four other criteria of cultural impact were also considered in the study: censorship and notoriety (for example, the controversy surrounding *A Clockwork Orange* (1971)), quotations and references in other media (such as *The Simpsons* (Fox, 1989–)), '*zeitgeist* moments' where films have captured the spirit of the times (*Bend It Like Beckham* (2002) inspiring the creation of an all-girls football team in India, for example) and 'cumulative impact' – the influence of films in changing attitudes over time (the report gives the example of Simon Callow's character Gareth in *Four Weddings and a Funeral* (1994) changing attitudes towards the gay community) (Narval Media et al. 2009: 10).

Revealing though these measurements were, *Stories We Tell Ourselves* drew conclusions about cultural impact without undertaking any research into audience perceptions of British films. This deficit was corrected two years later with a second study, *Opening Our Eyes*, published by the BFI after it assumed the functions formerly undertaken by the UKFC in 2011. *Opening Our Eyes* put audience responses at the centre of its approach. The study employed both qualitative and quantitative research methods, but was based mainly on interviews taken from 2,036 respondents aged from fifteen to 74 years. This research attempted to grapple with issues such as why people watch films, in what ways they value films and how films contribute to British identity and culture. As such, the study focused more on the value of film as a cultural experience rather than on the media impact of particular films over time.

Beyond considerations of how film is popularly valued and the longevity of the cultural impact that films can sustain, there are other measures of cultural worth which are more selective. What about notions of cultural value attributed to films by institutions like the BFI? These include specialised films (that is, foreign-language, documentary and British independent films), which are which are considered artistically important and stylistically innovative, or those which deal with pressing social or political issues (for example, the experiences of ethnic minorities and those living in poverty); such films may be considered worthy but are not necessarily popular. Sally Hibbin and Karen Alexander have insisted on the importance of encouraging under-represented film-makers to tell their stories, stating that a key problem lies with access to audiences (Aylett 2005: 348). Both identify the vital role of film education in growing new audiences for specialised films, though they agree that more thought needs to be given to the practicalities involved.

Considerations of cultural value were enshrined in Channel 4's defining remit to cater to unrepresented taste communities, to give airtime to minority voices and to offer alternatives to dominant television culture, although arguably such principles have since been challenged by the commercial realities of its business model in a multi-channel television marketplace. One of the purposes of this article is therefore to explore the ramifications of these conflicted definitions of cultural value in terms of the legacy of Channel 4's feature film output.

The processes by which films come to be valued as the best examples of a national cinema, a specific genre, a director's work or a studio's output and thus part of an established canon are complex. However, there are identifiable factors which influence these processes. The idea of a Film4 canon is of itself a marker of cultural worth; consensus about the film titles which might appear on this list reveals much about the prejudices of the arbiters, but also about perceived values that Film4 productions enshrine. Canon formation can be seen as an ongoing process of negotiation between notions of commercial and cultural value. It is selection, however, which is at the heart of canon formation. According to Janet Staiger: 'In purely practical terms, a scholar of cinema cannot study every film ever made. Selection becomes a necessity and with selection usually comes a politics of inclusion and exclusion. Some films are moved to the centre of attention; others to the margins' (1985: 8).

Staiger outlines typical rationales for selection and discusses the problems with each. The first rationale she outlines is 'efficiency'. A movie critic, writer or academic may give the example of one well-known and instantly recognisable film in order to illustrate a point succinctly. However, the problem is that this can give weight to one particular film over others of its kind. For example, academics and critics often cite *East Is East* when discussing British films which illustrate the experiences of ethnic minorities in the UK. However, Gurinder Chadha's *Bhaji on the Beach* (1993) is less frequently referenced, while films like Po-Chih Leong's *Ping Pong* (1986) and Mike Newell's *Soursweet* (1988) are almost never mentioned at all.[2]

Staiger's second rationale is the idea of 'putting order into chaos' (ibid.: 9). This involves grouping films of a particular period or on a specific theme under one heading (for example American horror or realist drama), with a few examples commonly chosen to stand in for the group. In this way *A Room with a View* (1985), *Maurice* (1987) and *Howards End* (1992) became synonymous with Channel 4's contribution to British heritage drama. The third rationale outlined by Staiger is that of 'evaluative selection' – the foregrounding of works which are seen to promote social or public good. It is in this area of canonisation (the application of cultural value outlined above) that politics is most keenly involved, as such value judgements are rarely free of 'self-interest and hegemonic influence' (ibid.: 10).

Lists of the best or most influential films are therefore always the product of personal interpretation, stylistic economy, institutional politics, cultural hegemony, critical consensus and any number of complex value judgements. To recognise and critically interrogate the range of individual or institutional forces at play, it is crucial to ask 'who makes the value judgments, and on what basis do they make those judgments?' (Long 2006: 34). What are the criteria for selecting a 'culturally influential' film? Moving beyond these general abstract concerns, the selection and positioning of Channel 4 productions in lists of top films provide a tangible point of focus for exploring canon formation in practice, for investigating perceptions of 'value', and therefore for thinking about the impact of Film4 on British film culture.

'Top film' lists and the importance of contemporaneous consecration in canon formation

In 1998, the BFI invited 1,000 professionals among the UK's film community to choose 100 films that were 'culturally British'. BFI staff initially selected 309 films for respondents to choose from, but other films could also be nominated. Although over 500 additional films were suggested, only two made it into the final list (*A Clockwork Orange* and *Small Faces* (1996)) (Lampel and Nadavulakere 2009: 242). The list was essentially a means of evaluating those films that were perceived, by experts and industry professionals, to be most culturally significant to British cinema based on the criteria suggested. Where they appear in the list, films funded by Channel 4 can thus be considered as productions which have helped make the greatest contribution to British cinema, by dint of being selected. However, it is important to bear in mind here that this list is from 1999, and does not include more recent examples. Furthermore, historical lists with a broad timeframe may be likely to exclude recent examples in favour of established classics.

In many ways, canonisation is synonymous with retrospective consecration, the process by which institutions confer legitimacy on a symbolic product long after its initial release (as opposed to contemporaneous consecration, which relates to acclaim and financial success immediately following release). In *The Field of Cultural Production*, Pierre Bourdieu outlines three types of cultural legitimacy: 'specific' (conferred by peers or fellow producers of cultural works), 'bourgeois' (granted by institutions of the dominant class) and 'popular' (based on public acclaim) (quoted in Allen and Lincoln 2004: 874). Joseph Lampel and Shivasharan Nadavulakere (2009) investigated the impact of contemporaneous consecration on retrospective consecration in the British film industry, drawing upon Bourdieu's original definition and applying it to the BFI Top 100 list. Lampel and Nadavulakere outline three ways in which a film can be contemporaneously consecrated: 'expert', 'peer' and 'market', with 'expert' related to festivals, 'peer' to industry awards and 'market' relating to popularity and box-office receipts (ibid.: 240–3). Lampel and Nadavulakere's work will be deployed here in order to assess whether contemporaneous consecration in the form of box-office figures, festival prizes and industry awards (such as BAFTAs and Academy Awards) affects retrospective consecration, specifically in the case of Film4 productions.

Table 1 lists the Film4 films which appear in the BFI Top 100 list, along with lists of BAFTA awards, box office figures and festival accolades (reflecting Lampel and Nadavulakere's criteria). Certain conclusions might also be drawn here about how far contemporaneous consecration directly affected the television viewing figures of Film4 films, many of which would have been broadcast on the channel some time after their initial theatrical run.

Given the methodology behind the BFI Top 100 list, what Table 1 shows is the often polarised relationship between peer/professional and institutional/expert consecration. As previously noted, the BFI 100

Table 1. Films with Channel 4 funding from the BFI 'Top 100' list

Film title (and number on the list)	Percentage of C4 funding	BAFTA (peer consecration)	The 'big three' festivals: Cannes, Venice and Berlin (expert)	Box office UK (millions) (market)	Viewing figures on first tx (millions)
10. *Trainspotting*	99	Best Adapted Screenplay (John Hodge) Alexander Korda Award for Outstanding British Film	None	12.40	4.6
23. *Four Weddings and a Funeral*	30	Best Actor in Leading Role (Hugh Grant) Best Supporting Actress (Kristin Scott Thomas) David Lean Award for Achievement in Direction (Mike Newell) Best Film	None	27.70	12.4
26. *The Crying Game*	33	Alexander Korda Award for Outstanding British Film	None	2.00	4.1

Table 1. Continued.

Film title (and number on the list)	Percentage of C4 funding	BAFTA (peer consecration)	The 'big three' festivals: Cannes, Venice and Berlin (expert)	Box office UK (millions) (market)	Viewing figures on first tx (millions)
40. *Secrets and Lies*	32	Best Actress in a Leading Role (Brenda Blethyn)	Cannes: Best Actress (Brenda Blethyn)	1.96	2.9
		Best Original Screenplay (Mike Leigh)	Palme d'Or		
		Alexander Korda Award for Outstanding British Film	Prize of the Ecumenical Jury		
42. *The Madness of King George*	31	Best Actor in a Leading Role (Nigel Hawthorne)	Cannes: Best Actress (Helen Mirren)	4.60	4.9
		Alexander Korda Award for Outstanding British Film			
		Best Make-up and Hair Award (Lisa Westcott)			

Table 1. Continued.

Film title (and number on the list)	Percentage of C4 funding	BAFTA (peer consecration)	The 'big three' festivals: Cannes, Venice and Berlin (expert)	Box office UK (millions) (market)	Viewing figures on first tx (millions)
50. *My Beautiful Laundrette*	100	None	None	0.75	4.3
67. *Mona Lisa*	15	Best Actor in a Leading Role (Bob Hoskins)	Cannes: Best Actor (Bob Hoskins)	?	7.8
71. *Elizabeth*	7	Best Actress in a Leading Role (Cate Blanchett) Alexander Korda Award for Outstanding British Film Anthony Asquith Award for Film Music (David Hirschfelder) Best Cinematography (Remi Adefarasin) Best Make-up and Hair (Jenny Shircore)	Venice: Max Factor Award (Jenny Shircore)	5.50	3.8

Table 1. Continued.

Film title (and number on the list)	Percentage of C4 funding	BAFTA (peer consecration)	The 'big three' festivals: Cannes, Venice and Berlin (expert)	Box office UK (millions) (market)	Viewing figures on first tx (millions)
73. A Room with a View	10	Best Actress (Maggie Smith) Best Supporting Actress (Judy Dench) Best Costume Design (Jenny Beavan, John Bright) Best Film Best Production Design (Gianni Quaranta, Brian Ackland-Snow)	None	2.50	4.0
80. The Draughtsman's Contract	50	None	None	0.42	2.1
82. Distant Voices, Still Lives	53	None		0.48	1.2
85. Brassed Off	57	None	None	3.30	4.9
91. My Name Is Joe	22	None	Cannes: Best Actor (Peter Mullan)	0.95	1.0
93. Caravaggio	54	None	Berlin: Silver Bear Award	0.24	1.8
95. Life Is Sweet		None	None	0.53	3.6

were voted for by industry professionals based on an initial list of 309 films drawn up by staff at the BFI. Lampel and Nadavulakere argue the BFI 100 were thus likely to be more affected by popular contemporaneous consecration (while the 309 were more likely to be weighted in favour of historical 'classics'), and perhaps the eventual line up of these titles reflects the joint industry-BFI selection processes (ibid.: 243). For example, there is a distinct demarcation between those populist, profitable films near the top of the list, which seem to correlate closely with critics' best films lists published in the popular press, while lesser known, less commercially profitable films by established auteurs such as Peter Greenaway and Terence Davies can be found further down the table. The films towards the top of the list (the 'most influential') have all won prestigious industry awards, with festival awards seemingly less important: for example, *Four Weddings* and *Trainspotting* were consecrated professionally and popularly, but not 'expertly' (that is, by cultural institutions).

Conversely, what about films like *My Name Is Joe* (1998) and *Life Is Sweet* (1990), which did not win significant awards at the time of their release but which are listed in the Top 100? Allen and Lincoln argue that films by established auteurs are more likely to be retrospectively consecrated by cultural institutions (2004: 878). Derek Jarman's *Caravaggio* (1986) appears in many top films lists but did not make significant box-office returns and garnered low viewing figures on television broadcast. Indeed, *The Draughtsman's Contract* (1982), *Distant Voices, Still Lives* (1988) and *My Name Is Joe* received very little popular recognition at the time of release, but were made by directors considered to be established auteurs and have since been appraised by critics and academics as being artistically and culturally innovative. However, overall, contemporaneous consecration in the form of expert, peer and popular recognition is a significant factor in determining which films will be selected by critics and institutions and will thus retain a degree of hold on the public imagination. Since retrospective consecration, in the form of best films lists, goes some way towards determining which films are remembered, the processes behind retrospective consecration are important in assessing which Channel 4 films have been considered to have had an 'impact' culturally and which films are remembered, cited and studied.

Best films lists published in newspapers and film magazines can also provide a good indication of which Film4 films have been seen as being popular and/or culturally significant. Those films which appear most often in these lists, taken from polls carried out by four popular publications over a period of ten years, are: *A Room with a View,*

Trainspotting, *Naked* (1993), *Four Weddings and a Funeral*, *Secrets and Lies* (1996), *Sexy Beast* (2000), *24 Hour Party People* (2002), *28 Days Later* (2002) and *Hunger* (2008). It must be borne in mind that the methodology for film selection varied between each publication. For example, the *Time Out* Top 100 was compiled with suggestions from '150 top industry professionals', while *Total Film* polled suggestions from just 25 critics. Nonetheless, the aggregation of these poll results outlined in Table 2 gives a useful indication of those Film4 productions considered by critics to have been influential in British cinema. The films here are ranked by the most popular first, with the accompanying numbers in this list indicating the position of each film in the original poll.

Christopher Long somewhat flippantly suggests that the larger the number of critics participating in a poll, the more likely *Citizen Kane* (1941) will poll at number one, suggesting a formula where x = number of critics and y = *Citizen Kane* polling at number one, and the likelihood of y increases with x (2006: 34). Such a formula may have a basis in reality when one considers that the Orson Welles film remained at number one in the *Sight and Sound* Top Ten Greatest Films poll from 1962 to 2002 (knocked down to number two only in 2012 by Yasujirô Ozu's *Tokyo Story* (1953)). In the conclusion to his book *Essential Cinema*, Jonathan Rosenbaum (2004) seeks to rectify problems inherent in canonisation by providing his own list of 1,000 greatest films in an attempt to challenge the established consensus. In relation to this, Long argues that:

> Consensus only breeds mediocrity or, if you prefer, more consensus... Such polls can only produce canons which include the same narrow set of masterpieces time and again. Ask each individual in the group what his top choices will be and you are far more likely to see greater diversity in the results, but the most idiosyncratic results are drowned out by mass consensus. (2006: 34)

By this reckoning consensus breeds consensus, which results in a diversity of other works languishing in obscurity. An example of this would be the over-representation of *Trainspotting* in critics' polls and academic work, which arguably detracts from the varied output of Film4 in the 1990s. By continually focusing on a small selection of 'great' productions, consensus about the significance of these films grows and becomes established and entrenched at the expense of other valuable works.

Press evaluations of Film4, usually written to coincide with Channel 4's milestone anniversaries, have observed this tendency. According

Table 2. Culturally influential films with Channel 4 funding (selected from four critics' best British films lists)

Total Film 2004 (Top 50)	Empire 2011 (Top 100)	Time Out 2012 (Top 100)	Telegraph 2013 (Top 50)
4. *Trainspotting*	10. *Trainspotting*	3. *Distant Voices, Still Lives*	13. *Four Weddings and a Funeral*
10. *Naked*	12. *This Is England*	10. *Trainspotting*	34. *Naked*
15. *Sexy Beast*	13. *Distant Voices, Still Lives*	11. *Naked*	39. *Secrets and Lies*
26. *A Room with a View*	21. *Four Weddings and a Funeral*	33. *Secrets and Lies*	47. *Trainspotting*
34. *Four Weddings and a Funeral*	26. *Shallow Grave*	48. *Hunger*	
45. *My Beautiful Laundrette*	37. *28 Days Later*	49. *Gallivant*	
	44. *Sexy Beast*	56. *Caravaggio*	
	57. *My Name Is Joe*	72. *The Long Day Closes*	
	58. *Slumdog Millionaire*	74. *Four Weddings and a Funeral*	
	62. *Secrets and Lie*	88. *This is England*	
	65. *Hunger*	94. *24 Hour Party People*	
	76. *Naked*	97. *28 Days Later*	
	83. *A Room with a View*		
	92. *Four Lions*		
	97. *24 Hour Party People*		

Sarah Gristwood, writing in the *Independent*, 19 December 1997, at the time of Channel 4's fifteenth anniversary, the list of notable Film4s

> goes on almost indefinitely: *Trainspotting, Four Weddings and a Funeral, The Madness of King George, Secrets and Lies, Mona Lisa, The Crying Game, My Beautiful Laundrette, Wish You Were Here . . .* Of course, besides the famous success stories, their list includes an awful lot of lesser movies, the names of which have passed from memory.

There is a strong trend in the press of equating Film4's successes with a handful of films, with repetition abounding in different publications and the same titles being cited at milestone anniversaries.

Nevertheless, Channel 4's anniversaries provide a good way of surveying the established Film4 canon and analysing the rationales for film selection by critics. With this in mind, it is useful now to look at how Channel 4 has viewed its back catalogue through a study of two Film4 anniversary seasons; the tenth anniversary was broadcast on Channel 4 in January 1993, and the thirtieth was made available online through Film4 on Demand throughout November 2012. These two seasons provide an element of historical contrast which allows an insight into Channel 4's own processes of canon formation through scheduling, and into how the channel's motivations for promoting certain Film4 titles have changed over time.

Film4 'best of' seasons: a case study of two anniversaries

In January 1993, Channel 4 screened a season of Film4's 'Greatest Hits' as part of the channel's ten-year anniversary celebrations. Out of approximately 160 Film4 productions screened on the channel up to that point, thirteen were selected that were seen to be 'the most popular and successful Film on Four's to have emerged over the past decade, which proves how closely Channel 4 has been associated with the biggest recent successes of the British film industry'.[3] These were: *Wish You Were Here* (1987), *Mona Lisa*, *Dance with a Stranger* (1985), *A Room with a View*, *My Beautiful Laundrette*, *Letter to Brezhnev* (1985), *Another Time, Another Place* (1983), *Hope and Glory* (1987), *Drowning by Numbers* (1988), *Distant Voices, Still Lives*, *Angel* (1982), *Prick Up Your Ears* (1987) and *Paris, Texas* (1984).

The selection of films reveals an effort to be representative of Film4's output, and encompasses films from each type of film-making/genre strongly associated with Film4 throughout the 1980s: contemporary social issues, experimental art cinema, international cinema and the British historical film (both avant-garde and heritage). The list is also heavily weighted in favour of festival winners and those films which had garnered critical acclaim and international recognition, and focuses on showcasing Film4's cultural achievements (particularly those films which had made an impact in the European art-house market).

It is worth noting that this anniversary fell within a period of transition, between the less commercially oriented Channel 4 of the 1980s and the more competitive environment of the early 1990s, as the channel moved towards selling its own advertising airtime in 1993. At this point, Film4 had also faced an eighteen-month hiatus between the departure of David Rose and the arrival of David Aukin as Head of Drama. The future of Film4 was uncertain during this period, with executives at the channel deliberating whether to continue funding feature films or to divert this money into TV series. Aukin[4] states that there may have been a hint of desperation behind the decision to promote this season, due in part to the uncertainty around Film4's future, which was compounded by its lack of recent success.

However, Film4 soon became commercially and culturally significant to Channel 4's brand identity. Catherine Johnson (2012) argues that in the 1990s broadcasters like the BBC and Channel 4 began to make use of branding strategies as a means of survival in the new commercial market. In the early 1990s Film4 was taking its first tentative steps towards focusing more on brand recognition, audience research and advertising,[5] which can be seen as part of an ongoing process of commercialisation that was taking hold at the channel. Indeed, Aukin ushered in a new era of market awareness and more ratings-driven programming, which influenced the decision to include film in the channel's rebranding toward the mid-1990s. The position of Film4 was also strengthened with the success of films like *Shallow Grave* (1994), *Four Weddings and a Funeral* and *Trainspotting*. According to Aukin, 'in the same way as Channel 4 news... there are certain things that branded Channel 4, and Film4 became one of those'.[6]

In November 2012, Film4oD ran a promotion entitled '30 films for 30p' as part of the channel's thirtieth anniversary celebrations. This season was not broadcast on the free-to-air Film4 channel. Instead, throughout November, a different film was made available each day on the Film4oD website for 30p, with the intention of promoting the channel's online platforms. The website stated in its promotional material:

> Film4 is celebrating its 30th anniversary by giving you the chance to watch 30 of its most iconic films from the past 30 years for just 30p per film. From the 1st November a different film from Film4's back catalogue will be available to rent for 30p each day from Film4oD, so you can rediscover great films you know, and discover great films you don't. The 30 films showcase some of the very best in British film making from the past 30 years.

The tenor of this statement is interesting in relation to the Film4 brand. According to a report into Channel 4's impact on the UK film industry by Olsberg SPI, in a crowded and fragmented sector the channel has a 'clear and distinctive brand, built over a 25-year period of commitment and innovation' – a brand which is hugely important to the British film industry because it is widely recognised, and as such attracts audiences and investment (2008: 20). Film4 is also important to Channel 4's own brand identity. Therefore, one would expect that film selections for this promotion would, to some extent, reflect how the channel wants to be seen in terms of its perceived impact on British cinema. However, the goal here was to promote the website, with the back catalogue being employed strategically to reinforce the Film4 brand and to extract value in the form of publicity. The films shown in Table 3 are not representative of the channel's film-making history, and do not need to be, which shows how the value of film to the channel and the identity of the Film4 brand has altered since its tenth anniversary, performing a different marketing function in a different set of circumstances.

Of course, it is important to remember that the channel could select only those films for Film4oD that they had the rights to screen. Film4oD is also hosted by FilmFlex, a third-party distributor, and the Film4 department does not have complete choice over the titles hosted on the Film4oD site, as Filmflex will choose those titles which it considers to be profitable to show. Bearing this in mind, it is possible to make certain observations about the films chosen for this promotion. For example, the season clearly shows a heavily contemporary focus: 21 of the 30 films were released in the 2000s, while the promotion included eight from the 1990s and just three from the 1980s (*My Beautiful Laundrette*, *Local Hero* (1983) and *Rita, Sue and Bob Too* (1987)). Some of the films chosen do appear regularly on the best films lists, but many more do not. The films chosen also foreground the importance of particular directors and styles to the channel's reputation for 'discerning, non-mainstream, alternative taste' (Olsberg SPI 2008: 19). Contemporary film-makers like Steve McQueen, Danny Boyle, Richard Ayoade and Ben Wheatley arguably appeal to a predominantly young audience with cine-literate and discerning interests in independent, non-mainstream cinema. Aside from the inclusion of directors Ken Loach and Mike Leigh, established British film-makers from the 1980s and 1990s are absent from the list.

Overall, the '30 films for 30p' promotion projects Film4's role as a producer involved in risky, innovative, alternative and above all contemporary film-making. There is a paradox here. It might be argued that Channel 4's film output in the 1980s demonstrated risk-taking, innovation and a freedom to experiment which is less evident today because of market imperatives. Yet, in the '30 films for 30p' promotion, it was necessary to claim the currency of these cutting-edge credentials by downplaying the past. Cultural amnesia is an important part of memorialisation, as the next section demonstrates.

Table 3. Titles in Film4's '30 films for 30p' promotion, November 2012

Title	Date available
My Beautiful Laundrette (1985)	1 November
Slumdog Millionaire (2008)	2 November
Nowhere Boy (2009)	3 November
Four Lions (2010)	4 November
Raining Stones (1993)	5 November
Genova (2008)	6 November
The Last King of Scotland (2006)	7 November
Me And You And Everyone We Know (2005)	8 November
Hunger (2008)	9 November
East Is East (1999)	10 November
Career Girls (1997)	11 November
Looking for Eric (2009)	12 November
Garage (2007)	13 November
Local Hero (1983)	14 November
Happy-Go-Lucky (2008)	15 November
127 Hours (2011)	16 November
This Is England (2006)	17 November
The Motorcycle Diaries (2004)	18 November
The Future Is Unwritten – Joe Strummer (2007)	19 November
Secrets and Lies (1996)	20 November
Brick Lane (2007)	21 November
Kill List (2011)	22 November
Attack the Block (2011)	23 November
Submarine (2011)	24 November
Sexy Beast (2000)	25 November
Brassed Off (1996)	26 November
Rita, Sue and Bob Too (1987)	27 November
Dead Man's Shoes (2004)	28 November
Tyrannosaur (2011)	29 November
Trainspotting (1996)	30 November

Forgotten films and the importance of DVD and third-party distribution

The exploitation of film back-catalogues on DVD and VoD, depending on how well they are marketed, can serve to give neglected or forgotten titles a new lease of life, long after the original television broadcast or cinema showing. Any discussion about the cultural impact of film, about how films are viewed by professionals, by institutions and by the public, is necessarily grounded in practicalities. A film may be stylistically innovative or culturally worthy but if it does not gain wide theatrical distribution and is not released and promoted in ancillary markets, it is not seen and does not become culturally relevant. However, DVD re-releases can help to reintroduce older films to new audiences, and can even lead to positive reappraisals of certain films. The UKFC study *Stories We Tell Ourselves* reported in its findings that:

> The arrival of cable and satellite platforms, and the success of video followed by DVD, have multiplied the pathways to a film-hungry audience. The DVD re-issue market, in particular, has led to a revival of interest in works by British film directors whose cultural impact had initially been limited due to having only small releases followed by occasional television screenings. (Narval Media et al. 2009: 10)

The popularity of older Film4s to some extent depends on distribution through these platforms. In 1987, Channel 4 funded Mike Newell's *Soursweet*, a film which explored the experience of a Chinese family living in London. After Leong Po-Chih's *Ping Pong*, this was one of only two Film4s to look closely at Chinese culture in Britain in the 1980s. The film follows a married couple, Lily and Chen, as they move to the UK to realise their dream of opening a take-away restaurant. When one considers that so few British films document the experiences of ethnic minorities struggling to reconcile their own identities with British life, it becomes clear that this film might be worthy of attention. After achieving limited impact upon release and remaining forgotten for over 20 years, *Soursweet* was released as part of Guerrilla Film's 'Forgotten Classics' collection in 2008. But what of *Ping Pong*?

At the Channel 4 and British Film Culture conference held at the BFI Southbank in November 2012, Felicia Chan and Andrew Willis presented a paper which focused on canonisation, and in particular on the ways in which certain Channel 4 films have been offered recognition at the expense of other potentially valuable productions. Although they welcomed the fact that *Soursweet* had gained a post hoc DVD release, they argued that *Ping Pong* was actually the better film since it engaged more effectively with Chinese culture and identity in the UK.[7] However, although DVD releases can offer a second life to a neglected film, selections for reissue are often determined by commercial rather than cultural judgements.

Here again, the channel's role in its own canon formation differs significantly from that of critics' polls (and from the BFI) in that it is motivated and restricted by a number of practical issues. In the case of the Channel 4 film catalogue, the availability of titles for DVD re-release is subject to complex factors. For example, the channel may have funded many films which are considered 'great British films', or distinctively 'Channel 4 films', but the channel may not own the rights to these productions, and therefore cannot release them as part of the 4DVD label (*Four Weddings and a Funeral* being one such example). Where the channel owns the rights to the films it has funded, it is able to make these rights available to a third-party distributor. However, the cost of releasing a DVD is often very high, making little-known films a potentially risky and unprofitable venture. Jessica Levick, responsible for overseeing the Film4 rights catalogue, states that there is a definite impetus on the part of the channel to exploit older, forgotten titles, but that it is often difficult to secure the interest of third-party distributors.[8] In order to secure DVD releases, Levick's department will typically draw up a list of films to which third-party rights are available and offer these to distributors. However, distribution is limited by the number of films those companies can release each year and the availability of other film catalogues to choose from.

Film4 DVD releases are also not guaranteed through 4DVD. Although the company carries around 120 of the channel's film titles, there are many more that they cannot release in a cost-effective way. The channel still has a responsibility to try and secure releases for films, although in some cases distributors will get in touch with Levick's department directly. For example, David Wilkinson of Guerrilla Films contacted the channel in order to select film titles for his 'Forgotten Classics' DVD label, and was interested particularly in those titles which had not had a release for many years. The titles chosen were Mike Newell's *The Good Father* (1985), Colin Gregg's *We Think the World of You* (1988), *Soursweet* and Christopher Morahan's *Paper Mask* (1990). According to Levick, Guerrilla wanted to release more titles but clearance issues were prohibitive. 'Forgotten Classics' provides an interesting example of a third-party distributor being specifically interested in older, marginalised titles with niche market value. Thus the likelihood of older films being given a second life on DVD depends on a combination of the channel pushing for the release of certain titles and the needs of third-party distributors, as well as the costs of a DVD release. The likelihood of forgotten films being reconsecrated also depends on critical and academic re-evaluation, which can be exemplified by the work carried out by Chan and Willis to incorporate previously marginalised films into the Film4 canon.

Special edition DVD and Blu-Ray box sets have also provided an avenue for the release of older, less well-known Film4 titles, as Levick states:

> If we can get a film distributed by Criterion in the USA, we will because
> [of] the way they package the DVDs – the way they create the inserts that
> go inside; the packaging and the artwork... They get amazing people
> to do essays on the inside... it's like a new release model almost, where
> this DVD is a beautiful thing to own... almost like a coffee table book.[9]

Films can often be released as part of a box set showcasing the films of
a particular director (for example, Film4 might sell the rights to a Ken
Loach film to a third-party distributor for their release of a collector's
edition box set). Although they may not be specifically referenced
as being Film4s, films funded by Channel 4 can be packaged and
distributed by director, company or theme, and can thus gain a limited
appeal among film fans and collectors. Indeed, the release of such box
sets in itself can be seen as another contribution to canon formation.

Current film releases can also have an impact on the reappraisal
of older, less well known films. For example, Levick states that she has
sought to remind distributors of Daniel Day Lewis's role in *My Beautiful
Laundrette* on the back of his Oscar nomination for Spielberg's *Lincoln*
(2012) and flagged up the rights availability of Pat O'Connor's *A Month
in the Country* (1987) following Colin Firth's nomination for *The King's
Speech* in 2011. In this way, reclamation of past Film4 productions can
be dependent on current successes in the industry, and the popularity
of contemporary productions can determine which marginalised films
return to the spotlight. The canon is, in some ways, constantly shifting
according to market forces, third-party distribution and current trends
in the British film industry. Indeed, although a handful of the same
titles can be (and have been) continually used by critics to sum up
Channel 4's cultural contribution to British cinema, the cultural impact
of the Film4 canon is also in constant flux, depending on the continued
circulation of lists, titles and personalities.

Conclusion

This article has shown the processes whereby certain Film4 productions
have come to be regarded as culturally significant and as representing
the best of the Channel 4 film catalogue, through critical appraisals,
consecration by cultural institutions, box-office popularity, industry
recognition and the channel's own promotional activities. Each
canonical list is constituted differently by various interests (press, critics
and institutions) and each is constituted with differing motivations.
Through a study of the ways in which contemporaneous consecration
(the popularity and critical acclaim of a production following its

release, measurable through industry awards, festival accolades and box-office receipts) can influence canon formation, it is possible to note certain trends in terms of the types of productions which commonly appear in the lists of best films, with those films which were popular upon their initial release better able to stand the test of time. Press and critical canonisation (articles published around Channel 4's major anniversaries as well as lists of top films) can offer a snapshot of which Channel 4 productions are commonly referred to in popular discourse, perhaps at the expense of other, less well-known titles. These processes of canonisation do not exist in isolation but are influenced by a number of complex factors (for example, many titles listed in polls carried out by newspapers and film magazines also appear in BFI lists of best films). Channel 4 is also responsible for building the identity of the Film4 canon, particularly in regard to its own milestone anniversary seasons. Interestingly, Channel 4's foregrounding of specific film titles in these seasons correlates with lists of top films, but only up to a point. With its highly contemporary focus, it can be argued that the '30 films for 30p' promotion was used as a marketing ploy in order to appeal to predominantly young, cine-literate audiences rather than as a means of showcasing Channel 4's historical contribution to British cinema. Finally, this article has explored the ways in which forgotten films can achieve reappraisal through DVD and VoD releases. Marginalised film titles can find outlets through third-party distribution (though this is highly dependent on commercial rather than cultural interests) and can even achieve recognition based on current trends in the film industry. Although most commentators would agree that Channel 4's films have had a significant impact on British film culture, these findings illustrate that the Film4 canon is far from established and can be contested on a number of levels. Indeed, in many small and surprising ways it is constantly in flux.

Acknowledgements

I am grateful to David Aukin and Jessica Levick for their interviews and to Rosie Gleeson and Evike Galajda at Channel 4 for archival assistance.

Notes

1. Film4 has gone through many name changes since 1982. Until 1998 Channel 4's films were commissioned by the Drama Department under the name Film on Four. Between 1998 and 2002 the channel's film production was the responsibility of FilmFour Ltd, a commercial subsidiary of the main channel. From 2003, Film4 was reincorporated within the channel's Drama Department. Though this article predominantly refers to the years 1982–98, for the purposes of coherence the

current term Film4 will be used throughout to describe the channel's feature films since 1982.

2. Felicia Chan and Andrew Willis, 'Missed, Lost and Forgotten Opportunities: *Ping Pong* and *Soursweet*', conference paper presented at the Channel 4 and British Film Culture Conference, BFI Southbank, 1 November 2012.

3. Channel 4 Press Information Pack, 2–8 January 1993, p. 31.

4. Personal communication with the author, 23 February 2012.

5. 'Film on Four reports', unpublished internal document, Channel 4.

6. Personal communication with the author, 23 February 2012.

7. Felicia Chan and Andrew Willis, 'Missed, Lost and Forgotten Opportunities: *Ping Pong* and *Soursweet*', conference paper presented at the Channel 4 and British Film Culture Conference, BFI Southbank, 1 November 2012.

8. Personal communication with the author, 11 January 2013.

9. Ibid.

References

Allen, M. P. and Lincoln, A. E. (2004), 'Critical discourse and the cultural consecration of American films', in *Social Forces*, 82: 3, pp. 871–94.

Aylett, H. (2005), 'Reflections on the cultural value of film', *Journal of British Cinema and Television*, 2: 2, pp. 343–51.

Johnson, C. (2012), *Branding Television*, London: Routledge.

Lampel, J. and Nadavulakere, S. S. (2009), 'Classics foretold? Contemporaneous and retrospective consecration', *Cultural Trends*, 18: 3, pp. 239–48.

Long, C. (2006), 'Revising the film canon', *New Review of Film and Television Studies*, 4: 1, pp. 17–35.

Narval Media/Birkbeck College/Media Consulting Group (2009), *Stories We Tell Ourselves: The Cultural Impact of UK Film 1946–2006 – A Study for the UK Film Council*, London: UKFC.

Northern Alliance and Ipsos MediaCT (2011), *Opening Our Eyes: How Film Contributes to the Culture of the UK*, London: BFI.

Olsberg SPI (2008), *Channel 4's Contribution to the UK Film Sector*, London: Olsberg.

Rosenbaum, J. (2004), *Essential Cinema: On the Necessity of Film Canons*, Baltimore, MD: Johns Hopkins University Press.

Staiger, J. (1985), 'The politics of film canons', *Cinema Journal*, 24: 3, pp. 4–23.

Laura Mayne is a doctoral candidate and research assistant based at the University of Portsmouth. She is completing her thesis on the cultural and industrial impact of Film4 on British cinema as part of the 'Channel 4 and British Film Culture' project, and she has also published and presented widely on this subject.

Channel 4 and the Red Triangle: A Case Study in Film Curation and Censorship on Television

Justin Smith

Abstract:

This article charts the history of an experiment, conducted during the autumn and winter of 1986–7, in which Channel 4 trialled an on-screen visual warning symbol to accompany screenings of a series of international art-house films. The so-called 'red triangle' experiment, though short-lived, will be considered as a case study for exploring a number of related themes. Firstly, it demonstrates Channel 4's commitment during the 1980s to fulfilling its remit to experiment and innovate in programme form and content, in respect of its acquired feature film provision. Channel 4's acquisitions significantly enlarged the range of international classic and art-house cinema broadcast on British television. Secondly, it reflects contemporary tensions between the new broadcaster, its regulator the IBA, campaigners for stricter censorship of television and policy-makers. The mid-1980s was a period when progressive developments in UK film and television culture (from the rise of home video to the advent of Channel 4 itself) polarised opinions about freedom and regulation, which were greatly exacerbated by the press. Thirdly, it aims to shed light on the paradox that, while over thirty years of audience research has consistently revealed the desire on the part of television viewers for an on-screen ratings system, the UK is not among some forty countries that currently employ such devices on any systematic basis. In this way the history of a specific advisory experiment may be seen to have a bearing on current policy trends.

Keywords: Channel 4; IBA; NVALA; red triangle; special discretion required; warning symbol.

Journal of British Cinema and Television 11.4 (2014): 481–498
Edinburgh University Press
DOI: 10.3366/jbctv.2014.0230
© *Journal of British Cinema and Television*
www.euppublishing.com/jbctv

Justin Smith

Introduction

This article charts the history of an experiment, conducted during the autumn and winter of 1986–7, in which Channel 4 trialled an on-screen visual warning symbol to accompany screenings of a series of international art-house films. While much has been written about film censorship, the majority of this literature has tended to focus on the policy and regulation of film for theatrical or video/DVD release, usually concentrating on particular causes célèbres. This investigation, by contrast, looks at the regulation of film on television; it concerns institutional policy in relation to a curated season of films. The first section outlines Channel 4's commitment during the 1980s to fulfilling its remit to experiment and innovate in programme form and content in respect of its acquired feature film provision. It also explains contemporary tensions between the new broadcaster, its regulator the IBA, campaigners for stricter censorship of television and policy-makers. The second section focuses on the 'red triangle season' of films which brought these ideological tensions to a head and assesses the resultant audience research and public relations management. The third section surveys subsequent research findings about programme information and reflects on the red triangle experiment in terms of television regulation and the Film4 channel's current commitment to world cinema.

'More Channel Four Shockers'

Channel 4 enriched and enlarged film culture in Britain from 1982 not only through its original commissions for *Film on Four* and in the new work sponsored by its Independent Film and Video Department, but also through its broadcasting of acquired film content. The responsibility for building a comprehensive and quite original film library was shared between Leslie Halliwell (whose brief was Hollywood and classic film) and Derek Hill (who handled independent titles). Hill, a vigorous champion of independent cinema and opponent of censorship, had founded the peripatetic New Cinema Club (1967–73), worked as an art-house distributor during the 1970s and went on to run the Essential Cinema Club (1976–80) with support from the Institute of Contemporary Arts (Prothero 2000). He was recruited by Jeremy Isaacs (Channel 4's first chief executive) having met him at a party in Cannes. Appointed two years before the channel's launch in November 1982, Hill was largely responsible for expanding the channel's provision of art-house and world cinema in its early years–two critical categories which he did much to popularise with the channel's minority audience through his cosmopolitan tastes and curated film seasons. As Ieuan Franklin notes:

> Hill's purchases were immediately exhibited in a regular film strand called *World Cinema* and formed the basis of numerous film seasons, such as the Sunday matinee season *All-India Talkies* (January–April 1983). Hill bought films that British television audiences had never seen before, from Turkey, Greece, Japan, Latin America, Australasia, as well as Europe ... In 1984 C4 was the first television company in the west to include Indian popular films as a regular part of its programming and audience research proved that they covered a huge mainstream audience.[1]

It was perhaps inevitable, amid the prurient attention which Channel 4's programming received from sections of the British press during its first years on air, that Isaacs' interpretation of its public service remit to innovate and experiment with form and content was the subject of frequent scrutiny from many quarters. As early as 30 December 1982 the *Daily Star*'s banner headline announced 'More Channel 4 Shockers', and a strapline proclaimed: 'Now they buy gay films for showing uncut.' The titles in question were Derek Jarman's *Sebastiane* (1976) and Ron Peck and Paul Hallam's *Nighthawks* (1978). Channel 4's Press Office issued a hasty response stating that they had no plans to screen either film, while an outraged Tory MP called for the IBA to withdraw the channel's licence. The furore was sufficient for the schedulers to sit on both films until the autumn of 1985, when both were shown and the controversy was promptly reignited.

Much must be said for Isaacs' principled commitment and tenacity, both in defending himself and the channel in the media and before the IBA, and in his encouragement of colleagues like Derek Hill. Isaacs wrote to David Glencross, then Director of Television at the IBA: 'The viewers we serve do not wish to be cosseted and protected from what is challenging or unusual. They welcome it. They do not want television that is unadventurous, bland, conformist. They look to us to widen their choice.'[2] And in a recent interview Hill recalled Isaacs' trust and largesse: 'He said "Go out there and buy what you fancy", more or less. And I said, "What's the budget?", and he said, "Oh, details!" And at the end of the month I rang him up and said, "I'm afraid I've spent a million pounds", and he said, "Well done, keep going!"'[3] But while Isaacs' devil-may-care attitude may have reigned in private, publicly the press pursued its own vendetta with equal determination. This hostile climate prompted an imaginative response from Channel 4's schedulers.

The year 1985 saw British Film Year and, as part of its autumn season, Channel 4 commissioned *The Times'* respected film critic, David Robinson, to curate and present a season of international cinema selected from Hill's library of titles. The choice included familiar greats such as Yasujirō Ozu's *Tokyo Monogatari* (1953), Akira Kurosawa's *Ikiru* (1952), Robert Bresson's *L'Argent* (1983) and Luchino Visconti's *Ludwig* (1972), but also the three feature films which Derek Jarman had then completed: *Sebastiane*, *Jubilee* (1977) and *The Tempest* (1979). This would be the first time that any of them had been shown on British television. *The Sunday Times* anticipated the controversy with barely disguised relish, provocatively noting on 20 October 1985 that:

> Channel 4 has decided to suffer the slings and arrows of outrage and show *Sebastiane*, Derek Jarman's film about the martyrdom of St Sebastian, which features Latin dialogue and homosexuality among Roman soldiers ... The IBA has approved the scheduling of the film with just one cut, a close-up of an erect phallus. Says a C4 spokesman: '*Sebastiane* had extremely good reviews and the IBA agreed to show it. I expect one or two people won't like it, but that's not an argument for not screening it.'
>
> Robinson's choice this Friday is also controversial: the movie *Nighthawks*, about a homosexual comprehensive school teacher, which was bought by C4 at the same time as *Sebastiane* and has not been screened before either.

Although the screenings were greeted in the tabloid press with the by then predictable degree of opprobrium, what is interesting here is the tactic of employing Robinson as the 'independent' arbiter of cultural value. In a pamphlet produced to accompany the season Robinson wrote: 'In one respect a guest selector has a considerable advantage over the official planners, who have to please week after week and can hardly answer back: "If you don't like it, there's a switch on your set, and you don't have to believe us next time we recommend something"' (1985: 1).

Although Robinson suggests he had a free hand in the film library, one admission is significant: 'I was encouraged to include the four British films in the selection precisely because they and their directors represent an important area of our native cinema that is unjustly and unwisely ignored by the commercial mainstream of production promoted by the current "British Film Year"' (ibid.). It was convenient indeed for Channel 4 that Robinson was 'a long-time champion of Jarman's work' (Peake 1999: 356), for it is clear that his intervention provided a means for the channel to screen 'difficult' films that they had acquired within the context of an independently curated season. Heavyweight critics of his repute certainly provided a welcome additional line of defence.

Less than a fortnight after *Sebastiane* had been broadcast, the *Guardian* reported on Conservative backbencher Winston Churchill's private members' Bill campaign to bring television and radio under the auspices of the Obscene Publications Act 1959, noting that: 'The Bill will mainly deal with the alleged obscene programmes on TV, such as the recent screening on Channel 4 of *Sebastiane*, which are causing growing concern among MPs. Mr Churchill believes his bill will have all-party support in the House and will win public sympathy.' This cause, which had been supported since the 1970s by a number of Conservative MPs and the National Viewers' and Listeners' Association (NVALA), had regained momentum in the wake of the passing of the Video Recordings Act 1984, itself the result of a tactical private members' Bill pursued by Conservative backbencher Graham Bright (Petley 2011: 23–32).

For her part, Mary Whitehouse, who headed NVALA, had already written to the IBA on 2 December 1985, enclosing copies of her organisation's monitoring reports on *Jubilee* and *Sebastiane*.[4] According to *The Times*, 4 December 1985, she claimed that the screening of these films had 'grossly offended against good taste and decency and could incite violence'. Although Churchill's Bill proceeded through the Commons at its second reading with a majority of 161 votes to 31, in order to ease its progress at the committee stage its architect had been forced to give ground on the so-called 'laundry list' of specific 'obscene' content it sought to bring under the law. Ministers clearly had little appetite to impose new controls on broadcasters; as junior Home Office minister David Mellor pointed out: 'Broadcasters were already under stricter obligations than those imposed by the 1959 Act. Their codes of guidance were strong and regularly reviewed, and the Home Secretary had recently reminded the BBC and IBA of the need to see that they were implemented' (quoted in the *Guardian*, 25 January 1986). Nonetheless, the broadcasters and their regulators began a very public show of robust reassurance by way of measured and dutiful response.

Thus the BBC announced in December 1985 that its committee of senior programme-makers responsible for drawing up its 32-page guidance notes on the portrayal of violence was to meet again to review the document in the New Year. On 4 March 1986 the *Guardian* reported that the IBA had let it be known that it would be examining 'all types of violence in its routine monitoring of television programmes'.

On 10 April 1986, it issued a press release reaffirming its commitment to its published Family Viewing Policy and stating its intention to draw clearer public attention to these guidelines by publishing them 'at regular intervals in the *TV Times*', placing 'an article explaining the policy' in the *TV Times* and using 'on-screen publicity'.[5] The IBA also took this opportunity to publish research it had conducted at the end of 1985 into audience responses to the Channel 4 film season Robinson's Choice, which had included the Jarman films. The *Guardian*, 4 March 1986, reported that this research showed that:

> Of the 126 people who claimed to have seen *Sebastiane*, 54 per cent said they disliked something about it, but only 29 per cent could explain what that was. Ten per cent said 'homosexuality,' 10 per cent said 'sex,' 42 per cent 'nudity' and 2 per cent 'bad language.' But the main objection to *Sebastiane* and *Jubilee* was that the viewers had not seen what they assumed the film to be. The motivation for seeing *Jubilee* was the wish to see a punk film with the music of Adam Ant. People had been disappointed. The main motivation for watching *Sebastiane* had been to see a period piece epic about Ancient Rome – *I Claudius* or *Ben-Hur* rather than sodomy. But very few people were willing to suggest that even *Sebastiane* should not have been shown as a late night film on television.

These responses were revealing. They showed that viewers (estimated to be 1,198,000 for *Jubilee* and 1,193,000 for *Sebastiane*) were not affronted so much as confused (BARB/Channel 4 1985).[6] Such evidence was sufficient for the IBA to urge Channel 4 to improve the effectiveness of its programme information in helping viewers to decide what to watch. As Barry Gunter of the IBA's Research Department observed, audience research 'indicated that despite on-air announcements and statements in *TV Times* about the content of certain late-night films, around half the viewers of such films reported that they were not aware of the particular nature of the material before they switched on.'[7] Discussions began at Channel 4 about how this might be remedied.

Meanwhile, on 25 April 1986, Winston Churchill's private members' Bill was defeated by a five-hour filibuster, led by Labour's Gwyneth Dunwoody, who, according to Alan Travis in the *Guardian*, 26 April 1986, said during the debate that 'the only evidence which the Bill's supporters had produced were two late-night Channel 4 films, *Jubilee* and *Sebastiane*, and a bizarre list which included many adjectives common on most shop floors'. She concluded: 'We are not here to write on to the statute book our own particular moral hang-ups. We are here to frame legislation that is sensible and balanced.' For the time being at least, good sense prevailed.

'C4 Unveils Its Sex Symbol'

The Broadcasting Act 1981, section 4(1)(a), required the IBA to 'satisfy themselves, so far as possible, that nothing is included in programmes which offends against good taste or decency or is likely to encourage or incite to crime or to lead to disorder or to be offensive to public feeling'. However, section 11(1) of the Act also imposed 'a duty on the Authority to ensure that programmes on Channel 4 contain a suitable proportion of matter calculated to appeal to tastes and interests not generally catered for by ITV; and to encourage innovation and experiment in the form and content of programmes'. Between the devil and this deep blue sea Channel 4 had, the IBA noted, 'from time to time transmitted important but often difficult films – generally from abroad – which have occasionally pressed very close to the absolute limits of acceptability under section 4(1)(a)'.[8]

The tightrope that Isaacs walked in balancing the terms of the Act became more precipitous in the wake of the controversy over *Sebastiane* and *Jubilee*. On 8 December 1985 he had told Sebastian Faulks, writing in the *Sunday Telegraph* about TV violence: 'Of course I worry about "accidental viewers" like children, but I think they are their parents' responsibility.' However, when he appeared on 29 November 1986 on the channel's viewer feedback programme, *Right to Reply*, to justify the screenings, he was less bullish in facing parental complaints. What, he was asked, if these late-night showings had been recorded on video in the home, and children had subsequently stumbled across the tape? What if an unprepared viewer accidentally lighted upon such explicit material in the course of channel-hopping? The challenge for Isaacs was 'how to screen more of the films on our list, which millions of viewers might want to see, without falling foul of the objection that some who ought not to see them or did not want to see them might inadvertently bump into them. I came up with the notion of the red triangle' (1989: 122).

In developing his idea Isaacs took counsel from the IBA. In an internal memo dated 16 July 1986, Colin Shaw wrote: 'I have no objections to another trial of use of the Warning Symbol by Channel 4 and the results of the research could prove useful. It would, of course, need to be preceded by a promotion explaining what it was and that might produce more reaction than the films themselves!'[9] As Shaw's memo indicates, the use of an onscreen warning symbol to accompany pre-transmission verbal warnings was not a new idea. At Thames Television Isaacs had produced the award-winning, 26-part series *The World at War* (ITV, 1973–4). Under an agreement with the IBA a warning symbol was introduced for the episode which dealt with the horrors of the Holocaust, broadcast on 27 March 1974.[10] And prior to this, a documentary called *Life by Misadventure: A Film about the Seriously Burned*, produced by Southern Television and broadcast on the ITV network, had been shown on 7 August 1973 with a small white outline rectangle in the lower left-hand corner of the screen throughout. A follow-up survey in the ATV area of the West Midlands revealed that '57% of respondents thought the scheme was a "very good idea" and another 32% felt it was a "good idea".'[11] Subsequent audience research was commissioned by the IBA in the ATV area following the 'Genocide' episode of *The World at War*. Dr J. M. Wober, deputy head of research at the IBA, reported to Barry Reeve, research and marketing services manager at ATV, that the research found that older people were less aware of the symbol, that fewer women than men disregarded the symbol, that 66 per cent would keep watching next time they saw a warning symbol, and that 'nearly everybody thinks the symbol is a good idea, which', he added wryly, 'may merely reflect how little of a good idea such a question is.'[12]

The red triangle warning symbol experiment ran on Channel 4 from 19 September 1986 to 7 February 1987 and was applied to ten films screened after 11.15 p.m. It took the form of a white triangle with a red border and was shown in a corner of the screen throughout the entire film. The symbol appeared with the words 'Special Discretion Required' before a film began and at the end of each advertising break. As David Glencross pointed out: 'There was no intention that the symbol be used with material that would not otherwise have been transmitted by Channel 4.'[13] But nonetheless, the IBA anxiously previewed all the films selected for the season and insisted upon a number of cuts.[14] For Hill, who curated the season, the symbol became (as Isaacs had hoped) a very useful way of packaging some of the art-house titles he had accumulated: 'The films were not acquired with such a season in mind. It was Jeremy Isaacs' idea to put them together in this way and proved a brilliant notion as it provoked controversy, effective publicity and considerably higher audiences than these films might otherwise have attracted.'[15]

The PR campaign, however, was not well managed. In advance of its official launch the news had been leaked to the press, and in the *Standard*, 14 August 1986, Isaacs was forced to defend the channel's commitment 'to allowing an individual opportunity to see particular works of individual artistic vision'. The *Mirror*, 15 August, also got in on the act, chortling: 'Eye, Eye! It's Sex on TV', as did its Sunday stablemate with 'Watch out for the Beasties', on 17 August. Then a suitably measured press release of 21 August 1986 announced: 'The channel is reluctant to cut the work of outstanding film directors, but it is equally concerned to alert viewers who might themselves be offended, or might wish to protect others in their families.' Isaacs was quoted here maintaining that 'viewers are capable of making informed choices themselves about what they watch. This symbol will help them choose and will also serve to warn those who come across one of these films unawares.'[16] But by this time the press response had already built up a head of steam. The *Standard*, 21 August, trumpeted: 'Triangle is TV's New Sex Symbol'; the same day's *Mail* announced 'C4 Unveils Its Sex Symbol'; the *Star*, 22 August, riffed on 'TV's Sex Triangle'; the same day's *Express* chimed in with: 'Warning! It's a TV Shocker'; and also on 22 August *Today* promised: 'Warning: Sex Scenes Will Appear'; and, a little later, on 18 September, the *Telegraph* advised readers to 'Watch out for TV's Symbolic Decline'. As Colin Shaw had anticipated and Hill recalled, the innovation attracted a level of attention (predicated on the appeal of sex rather than the repugnance of violence) that the films would not otherwise have gained, much to Isaacs' embarrassment. Mary Whitehouse immediately condemned the initiative as a cheap promotional stunt. On 15 August the *Mail* quoted her as complaining that 'it is simply a get-out for Channel 4 to enable them to keep on showing such films ... By doing this, they are advertising the programmes to the people whom they are supposedly trying to protect.'

The 'red triangle season' began with Claude Faraldo's critically acclaimed 'surreal black comedy' *Themroc* (1972), 'starring Michel Piccoli as a middle-aged worker who suddenly throws off all sexual, social and political inhibitions'.[17] It was broadcast uncut at 11.30 p.m. on 19 September 1986. Channel 4's press information movie notes remarked upon its novel substitution of conventional dialogue with an 'invented language', and praised the central performance of Piccolo 'who plays with a wildness and refreshing bonhomie that is contagious. But it is Faraldo's triumph in that he creates a memorable and credible universe of his own and brilliantly uses it to explore some of the stranger byways of human behaviour and aspirations.[18] However, in a report presented to the Parliamentary All-Party Media Group the NVALA described *Themroc* as 'one-and-a-half hours of unadulterated assault on the senses containing the glorification and enjoyment of mindless violence'.[19] And in the *Mail on Sunday*, 21 September 1986, in an article headed 'Mary Blasts "X" Film on TV', Whitehouse urged advertisers such as Sainsbury's, Cadbury and British Telecom to boycott Channel 4. On 27 September 1986, Isaacs appeared on the viewers' response programme *Right to Reply* to defend the experiment, concluding:

> Some do not want the symbol at all because it spoils their pleasure in viewing. I ask them to be patient and tolerant as we try to demonstrate that contemporary work that portrays life honestly and explicitly, and that has previously been thought by everyone else unsuitable for screening on television, can be successfully included in our schedule.[20]

At the IBA, an exasperated Robin Duvall wrote to Colin Shaw, asking: 'How can he say this?'[21] It was not, perhaps, Isaacs' finest hour in PR terms.

Subsequent films in the series continued to provoke criticism from the NVALA, while the response in the press became more muted as the season progressed. Shuji Terayama's *Sho o suteyo, machi e deyo* (*Throw Away Your Books, Let's Go into the Streets*) (1971) was broadcast on 10 October 1986. Adapted from Terayama's own stage play, the film, his first feature, was shown on Channel 4 the week after his 1974 film *Den-en ni shisu* (*Pastoral Hide and Seek*). Both had been subjected to minor cuts for violence at the request of the IBA.[22] Channel 4's movie notes championed Terayama's auteur status:

> Like *Pastoral Hide and Seek*, this film is semi-autobiographical, again scripted by Terayama and based upon his play and book of essays of the same name ... Fascinatingly, the film version contains echoes of the stage original, including the collage-style construction, unpredictable changes in tone, and direct address to the audience.[23]

Matters of aesthetics cut no ice with Whitehouse, however, who observed that this rite-of-passage drama 'had the recurring theme of anarchy, both moral and physical, and contained the prolonged and graphic attempted seduction of a virgin teenage boy by a woman prostitute.'[24] Another kind of teenage angst was the focus of the Dennis Hopper-directed *Out of the Blue* (1980), which was the penultimate offering in the season screened on 10 January 1987, in which a rebellious fifteen-year-old kills her dysfunctional and abusive parents.

The imaginative schedule also included three films by the German director Helma Sanders-Brahms. *Deutschland bleiche Mutter* (*Germany, Pale Mother*) (1980) and *Flügel und Fesseln* (*The Future of Emily*) (1984) were shown either side of *Die Berührte* (*No Mercy – No Future*) (1981), only the latter attracting the red triangle treatment for its stark examination of a female schizophrenic's alienation and abuse. It had won the best film award at the BFI London Film Festival in 1982 and was subsequently shown at the ICA. Institutional exposés of a different nature were provided by David Stevens' comedy-drama set in an Australian VD clinic (*The Clinic*, 1982), and by the concluding film in a short season of work by the late Turkish director Yilmaz Güney, *Duvar* (*The Wall*) (1983), which is a harsh indictment of the penal regime in Güney's homeland.

The radical Yugoslavian director Dusan Makavejev was represented in the series by his anarchic Anglo-Swedish comedy *Montenegro* (1981), starring Susan Anspach and Erland Josephson, notable for its use of Marianne Faithfull's bittersweet anthem of liberation, 'The Ballad of Lucy Jordan'. But Mrs Whitehouse was more preoccupied by a 'prolonged scene where a woman is entertaining everyone by singing and gyrating naked while a radio-controlled model tank, with an erect plastic penis sticking out of the barrel, is driven around her while she gyrates'.[25]

The Channel 4 press packs reveal that the red triangle films, which included the celebrated Antonioni's *Identificazione di una donna* (*Identification of a Woman*) (1982), were interspersed with other international offerings of equal stature which did not require the warning: Yaky Yosha's *Ha'ayit* (*The Vulture*) (1981), Ingmar Bergman's *Persona* (Sweden, 1966) and Yannick Bellon's *L'amour violé* (*Rape of Love*) (France, 1977), though the latter avoided the triangle presumably only because a gang rape scene was cut on the recommendation of the IBA. It is interesting to note here (as with the Terayama films) that despite Isaacs' claim that the symbol aimed (in part) to defend the integrity of auteurs by enabling their work to be shown uncut, the IBA continued to exercise its own judgement.

The IBA's caution, however, failed to avert criticism, not only from those of the Whitehouse persuasion but, under pressure from the NVALA, from advertisers too. *The Times*, 21 October 1986, reported that 'Bank of Scotland, Kelloggs, Hill Samuel and Sainsbury have … banned their products being advertised during the screening of such films.' Meanwhile, to liberal opinion the application of the symbol seemed equally ill-judged. The majority of complaints received by the IBA and Channel 4 concerned the intrusiveness of the on-screen symbol to the viewing experience. And, ironically, the symbol may well have been responsible for *The Clinic* and *Montenegro* (both sex comedy-dramas and the 'lightest' films in the selection) attracting viewing figures of 2.7million each – double the ratings for the David Robinson season.[26]

No sooner was the season over than the inquests began, on all sides. Channel 4 and the IBA produced their own market research reports, while the NVALA prepared a video of extracts together with screening notes for a presentation to the Parliamentary All-Party Media Group on 17 February 1987.[27] Isaacs responded by denouncing the showing of selected extracts out of context, and offered to re-show the films for MPs in their entirety. A *Times* headline noted on 12 February: 'Sex Films Draw Record Interest from MPs'. In the event a special screening of *Montenegro* was organised at Channel 4's Charlotte Street viewing theatre on 18 February 1987.[28] Channel 4 issued a carefully worded press release to accompany this Parliamentary scrutiny:

> The detailed information which Mary Whitehouse gives about such scenes tends to generate precisely the kind of sensational publicity that the channel itself has always responsibly avoided in its own information about the films. And while the channel needed to inform viewers, through press releases and on-air announcements, about the 'red triangle' experiment when it started in September, the sensational publicity surrounding the symbol was generated not by Channel 4, but by Mary Whitehouse's advance protests.[29]

While the double-edged sword of publicity remained the unwieldy weapon – if not of choice then of necessity – in the ongoing battle between freedom and censorship, behind the scenes the survey data was sifted and interpreted. The responses from the separate Channel 4 MAS Omnibus and the IBA BARB Top Panel surveys were collated and the following observations made. Firstly, 86 per cent thought the symbol was a good or very good idea. Of those who thought it was a bad or very bad idea, the majority objected on the grounds that it was 'an infringement of liberty rather than it encouraged people to watch unsuitable films (although this was the second most stated reason)'. Secondly, the research suggested that the symbol 'should be retained although confined to films rather than extended to other programmes'. Thirdly, 'the majority of people "use", or say they would use, the device of a symbol to switch away from the programme for the sake of themselves or others.' Finally, there was the problem that 'a significant proportion of people saw a film as a result of seeing it billed as an SDR . . . i.e. it attracted them to a programme they would not normally have watched.' In particular, the IBA survey found 'that there is a problem of 12–15 year olds viewing films in this way'.[30]

On 2 April 1987 Sue Stoessl, Channel 4's Head of Marketing, prepared a report on the findings for a meeting with the IBA on 1 May. Her conclusions were simple. The warning symbol should be retained for certain films on the basis of the survey support. The warning symbol should not be extended to other programmes since films were a special case: 'The low frequency of viewing suggests that gradually the viewing of SDR would reduce to that of other films in the slot. With programmes this would not happen as each one would be seen as a different possibility to view salacious material.'[31] Concerned by the adverse publicity which the symbol's use had attracted for 'difficult' material which was arguably only of minority interest, the IBA favoured dropping the warning pending further research. Isaacs, with the support of his board and figures that showed strong public endorsement of the experiment, was minded to retain the symbol, but 'to attempt to devise procedures to limit gratuitous publicity'.[32]

The IBA respected Channel 4's position, although David Glencross (1987) warned that reducing press attention was 'likely to prove difficult'.[33] That challenge is evidenced by no fewer than five drafts of a press release revealing the outcome of these deliberations in the Channel 4 archives. On 5 August 1987 the *Guardian* reported that a Channel 4 spokesman had conceded that while 'the symbol would be retained throughout at the top left-hand corner of all films whose sexual content, language or violence might offend some viewers, the triangle would not be shown in the *TV Times*, or on the screen until immediately before the film started.' And although Channel 4 'would still do its best to describe such films in pre-publicity', it had 'no plans for screening any such late night films in the current year's schedules'. In the event, temporary self-censorship appeared to be the best remedy for unwarranted press attention. Certainly, in the wake of Gerald Howarth MP's abortive 1987 attempt to revive the Obscenity Bill, various journalists wondered if broadcasters had lost their nerve. Taking the long view, Isaacs recalls the 'damned red triangle' as one of Channel 4's more ignominious innovations, 'which fortunately we could get rid of fairly soon'.[34]

A case study in television regulation

It may be fruitful to reflect upon this episode as a case study in television regulation. In 1995 the Broadcasting Standards Council commissioned new research, at an estimated cost of £60,000, which, as the *Guardian* reported on 8 December, found that '92 per cent of viewers wanted more information about programmes, and 40 per cent suggested on-screen symbols would help guide viewing decisions. Thirty-eight per cent wanted warning symbols in listings magazines.' But Colin Shaw, by then the Council's director, argued that broadcasters should proceed with caution, pointing out in the article that 'the red triangle and an earlier "black dot" experiment by the now defunct ATV were abandoned because they became a "turn-on" for viewers attracted to sexually explicit material. In an increasingly fragmented and multi-channel television environment it would be difficult to produce uniform standards and symbols.' In his own book on the subject of media ethics, Shaw produced fresh research from the United States, conducted in 1998, which 'indicated that the use of symbols can contribute to a reduction in the audience of the numbers of younger viewers watching a marked programme' (1999: 78). A joint report by the Broadcasting Standards Commission and the Independent Television Commission published in 2003 produced survey findings which indicated that a majority of respondents favoured the modification of current programme information by the addition of 'pre-transmission warnings and on-screen warnings' (Millward Hargrave 2003: 20). In 2006, Ofcom, the current UK media regulator, produced Programme Information Research about 'current attitudes and behaviours towards programme information' (Ofcom 2006: 32). It found that while opinion was divided about the adequacy of current UK television programme information, half the sample surveyed were attracted by ways of improving warnings about content. Three systems were compared, including text-based information, warning symbols and age ratings. It was felt by 46 per cent that text-based systems provided the best detail about programme content, but 30 per cent of respondents favoured the use of symbols particularly in relation to children's viewing.

Conclusion

Two conclusions emerge from this body of research. Firstly, the frequency with which broadcast regulators have returned to this agenda since the 1980s reinforces the concerns at the heart of this debate. Secondly, there are consistently significant levels of support – notwithstanding the transformation of television culture and technology – for enhanced programme information to provide viewer (and especially parental) guidance. Given these conclusions, why then is the UK not among the 40 or so countries which currently have such systems in place? Can anything be drawn from the lessons of Channel 4's red triangle experiment to help answer this question?

One answer might be that the quality of programme information has improved since the 1980s. Firstly, the end of the *Radio Times* and *TV Times* duopoly on television listings in March 1991 gave rise to an increase in the number of print sources for content information. Secondly, digital television technology has since enabled a range of programme information to be accessed on screen, and certain subscription services now operate their own ratings systems. Thirdly, in 2004 Ofcom published its consultation document *Strategy and Priorities for the Promotion of Media Literacy*, which saw the establishment of the Audio Visual Content Information Working Group, with the aim of improving the provision of programme information.

Another observation might be that the polarised terms of the ideological debates around television regulation, freedom and censorship which characterised the 1980s have since receded, giving way to more pragmatic responses to such matters. However, a different position on this might be that the power of the UK's tabloid press, which did much to fan the flames of the red triangle furore, continues to militate against any mature public debate about freedom and censorship (except, of course, when it affects their own practices – vide its uniformly hostile response to the recommendations of the Leveson Inquiry).

Finally, a cynic might conclude that regulation is now managed to some extent by the economics of the multi-channel market. Channel 4's proportion of foreign-language films shown remains higher than any other UK broadcaster.[35] However, can anyone seriously imagine the unremittingly harrowing account of Turkish prison life documented in Yilmaz Güney's *Duvar* being shown on the Film4 freeview channel? While its difficult themes of abuse and corruption remain all too relevant, it is hardly entertainment. If rank populism (and consumer access to a diverse film culture via DVDs and downloads) has squared the circle of the cinema-on-TV debate, this should not be seen as a victory for moral crusaders like Whitehouse. But it is a defeat for the idea of a curated film culture which, in the hands of enlightened enthusiasts like Isaacs, Hill and Robinson, broadened our access to and appreciation of what cinema could be, and educated a generation of cinephiles and cineastes. At a time when the BFI (2012), the UK's lead body for film, and the DCMS Film Policy Review Panel (2012) are united in putting film education at the forefront of priorities to increase and broaden the UK audience for film, this conclusion ought to give pause for thought.

In the light of this transformation, and by way of a postscript, Channel 4's recent nostalgic resurrection of the red triangle symbol in a marketing campaign entitled Born Risky, was ironic indeed.[36] Channel 4 may still be innovative in its programme commissions, but I don't see many risks being taken in the schedules of Film4.

Acknowledgements
This research draws upon original interviews with key personnel who were at the centre of the red triangle experiment at Channel 4 and the IBA: Sir Jeremy Isaacs, Paul Bonner, Derek Hill and Colin Shaw. It makes use of the Channel 4 Press Packs website produced in a partnership between the University of Portsmouth and the British Universities Film and Video Council as part of the AHRC-funded project 'Channel 4 and British Film Culture' (2010–14). I am also indebted to Rosie Gleeson, Information and Archives Manager at Channel 4, and to the BFI Library for access to the Independent Television Commission press cuttings database. This article has also benefited from invaluable research conducted on behalf of the project by Ieuan Franklin at the IBA archive at Bournemouth University, to whom we are grateful.

Notes

1. 'Building a Television Audience for World Cinema in the (Late) Era of Media Scarcity'. Paper presented at SCMS conference, Seattle, 2014.
2. Letter to David Glencross, 9 July 1985, IBA/ITA/CA archive, Bournemouth University.
3. Interview with Ieuan Franklin and Rachael Keene, 16 January 2013.
4. Letter to Lord Thomson of Monifieth, Chairman of IBA, 2 December 1985, *Scum* file, Channel 4 archive.
5. IBA press release, 'The IBA and Family Viewing Policy, The Obscene Publications (Protection of Children etc) Amendment Bill', 10 April 1986, Red Triangle file, Channel 4 archive.
6. BARB ratings, Derek Jarman file, Channel 4 archive.
7. Barry Gunter, *The Channel 4 Warning Symbol Experiment: Public Attitudes and Awareness*, 1987, IBA, pp. 1–2, IBA/ITA/CA archive, Bournemouth University.
8. David Glencross, *The Channel 4 Red Triangle Warning Symbol*, IBA Paper 112 (87), 17 July 1987.
9. Memo from Colin Shaw to David Glencross, 'Channel 4 films and warning symbol', 16 July 1986, IBA/ITA/CA archive, Bournemouth University.
10. Letter from J. M. Wober to Jeremy Isaacs, 16 May 1974, IBA/ITA/CA archive, Bournemouth University.
11. Barry Gunter, *The Channel 4 Warning Symbol Experiment: The IBA's and Channel 4's Results Compared*, 1987, report to the IBA, IBA/ITA/CA archive, Bournemouth University.
12. Letter from J. M. Wober to Barry Reeve, 8 May 1974, IBA/ITA/CA archive, Bournemouth University.
13. David Glencross, *The Channel 4 Red Triangle Warning Symbol*, IBA Paper 112 (87), 17 July 1987.
14. Memo from Robin Duvall to Colin Shaw, 16 September 1986, IBA/ITA/CA archive, Bournemouth University.
15. Interview with Ieuan Franklin and Rachael Keene, 16 January 2013.
16. Channel 4 Press Office, 'Channel 4 introduces warning triangle for late night films', 21 August 1986, Red Triangle file, Channel 4 archive.
17. Channel 4 Press Packs, programme listings: 1986 week 38 page 73; < http://beta.bufvc.ac.uk/new/c4pp/index.php/page/c4_pp_1986_38_0913_0919_073_proglist > (accessed 4 February 2013).
18. Ibid.

19. NVALA report on the red triangle films submitted to the Parliamentary All-Party Media Group, 17 February 1987, IBA/ITA/CA archive, Bournemouth University.
20. Memo from Robin Duvall to Colin Shaw, '*Right to Reply*: Warning triangle', 29 September 1986, IBA/ITA/CA archive, Bournemouth University.
21. Ibid.
22. Memo from David Glencross to John Whitney, 1 December 1986, IBA/ITA/CA archive, Bournemouth University.
23. Channel 4 Press Packs, 'Movie highlights: 1986 week 41 page 59'. < http:// bufvc.ac.uk/tvandradio/c4pp/search/index.php/page/c4_pp_1986_41_1004_1010_059_movhigh > (accessed 5 May 2014).
24. NVALA report on the red triangle films submitted to the Parliamentary All-Party Media Group, 17 February 1987, IBA/ITA/CA archive, Bournemouth University.
25. Ibid.
26. BARB figures reproduced in Channel 4 report, Red Triangle file, Channel 4 archive.
27. NVALA report on the red triangle films submitted to the Parliamentary All-Party Media Group, 17 February 1987, IBA/ITA/CA archive, Bournemouth University.
28. Channel 4 Press Office, invitation to MPs, 17 February 1987, Red Triangle file, Channel 4 archive.
29. Channel 4 press release, 17 February 1987, Red Triangle file, Channel 4 archive.
30. Sue Clench, internal memo with research report to Jeremy Isaacs, Paul Bonner, Sue Stoessl, 'SDR audience research', 29 January 1987, Red Triangle file, Channel 4 archive.
31. Sue Stoessl, *The Red Triangle Warning Symbol*, draft paper, 2 April 1987, Red Triangle file, Channel 4 archive.
32. Channel 4 Board minutes, minute 21, 23 June 1987, IBA/ITA/CA archive, Bournemouth University.
33. David Glencross, *The Channel 4 Red Triangle Warning Symbol*, IBA Paper 112 (87), 17 July 1987.
34. Interview with the author, 9 November 2010.
35. Channel 4 showed 35 of the 41 foreign-language films broadcast on UK network television in 2006, although this figure is a far cry from the proportion shown under Derek Hill's stewardship in the 1980s.
36. 'Channel 4 "born risky" by 4 Creative', < http://www.campaignlive.co.uk/thework/1217102/ > (accessed 5 May 2014).

References

British Film Institute (2012), *Film Forever: Supporting UK Film*, London: British Film Institute.
Film Policy Review Panel (2012), *A Future for British Film: It Begins with the Audience ...*, London: Department of Culture, Media and Sport.
Isaacs, J. (1989), *Storm Over 4: A Personal Account*, London: Weidenfeld & Nicolson.
Millward Hargrave, A. (ed.) (2003), *Broadcasting Standards Regulation*, London: Broadcasting Standards Commission/Independent Television Commission.
Ofcom (2004), *Ofcom's Strategy and Priorities for the Promotion of Media Literacy: A Consultation Document*, London: Ofcom.
Ofcom (2006), *Programme Information Research: An Investigation into Current Attitudes and Behaviours Towards Programme Information*, London: Ofcom.
Peake, T. (1999), *Derek Jarman*, London: Little, Brown.

Petley, J. (2011), *Film and Video Censorship in Modern Britain*, Edinburgh: Edinburgh University Press.

Prothero, D. (2000), 'Interview with Derek Hill', *Journal of Popular British Cinema*, 3, pp. 133–43.

Robinson, D. (1985), *Robinson's Choice: Films for Channel 4*, London: Comedia.

Shaw, C. (1999), *Deciding What We Watch: Taste, Decency, and Media Ethics in the UK and the USA*, Oxford: Oxford University Press.

Justin Smith is Reader in British Film Culture at the University of Portsmouth, UK. He is the author of *Withnail and Us: Cult Films and Film Cults in British Cinema* (I. B. Tauris, 2010) and, with Sue Harper, *British Film Culture in the 1970s: The Boundaries of Pleasure* (Edinburgh University Press, 2011). He was Principal Investigator on the AHRC-funded project 'Channel 4 Television and British Film Culture' (2010–14).

Film4, Freeview and Public Service Broadcasting: Screening Films on British Television in the Multi-channel Era

Rachael Keene

Abstract:

This article analyses the shift in programming policy that took place when Channel 4's specialist subscription channel FilmFour was relaunched as Film4 on the Freeview digital terrestrial television platform in 2006. Scheduling data is used to interrogate the nationality, age and genre of films screened on both channels between 1998 and 2011. The changing character of film programming during this period is shown to relate, in part, to increased commercial pressures brought about by the rapidly evolving multi-channel landscape. While commercial imperatives were indeed a key factor in this evolution, Film4's scheduling strategies are also shown to be a product of the broadcaster's desire to reassert its public service identity in the Freeview era.

Keywords: Channel 4; film on television; Film4; FilmFour; Freeview; public service broadcasting.

Introduction

During the early 2000s the British broadcasting landscape underwent a series of significant changes that would impact upon Channel 4's future film exhibition practices. The broadcaster's dedicated subscription film channel FilmFour had been in existence since 1998, and was available across the UK's television distribution platforms for a charge of £5.99 per month (£6 for ONDigital customers). However, in 2002 a BBC-led consortium achieved a licence agreement

Journal of British Cinema and Television 11.4 (2014): 499–516
Edinburgh University Press
DOI: 10.3366/jbctv.2014.0231
© *Journal of British Cinema and Television*
www.euppublishing.com/jbctv

that would allow a 24-channel free-to-air digital terrestrial television service to be launched. Writing in *The Times* on 5 July 2002, Raymond Snoddy argued that this development made the concept of a subscription channel run by a public service broadcaster completely untenable. The broadcasting sector also came under scrutiny from the British government during this period with the publication of the Communications Act 2003, section 265(3) of which reinforced the importance of Channel 4's remit and encouraged the continuation of a broadcasting strategy that simultaneously 'demonstrates innovation, experiment and creativity in the form and content of programmes' and 'appeals to the tastes and interests of a culturally diverse society' (2003: 237).

This interrogation of Channel 4's core public service values sparked an internal re-evaluation of the broadcaster's activities, particularly in relation to its expanding multi-channel portfolio. Writing in the company's 2004 annual report, Chief Executive Andy Duncan explained that 'Channel 4's role will become more, not less important in the multi-channel, multi-platform digital future. As the public service contribution of ITV and Five declines, we will become the only effective public service alternative to the BBC, providing real competition for them and, more importantly, real choice for viewers' (Channel Four Television Corporation 2004: 5).

While the Communications Act did not draw any explicit links between Freeview and public service broadcasting, it did set the scene for a review of Channel 4's subscription services, while the growth of multi-channel television increased the level of competition for viewers across the UK's core terrestrial channels. In November 2006 the subscription FilmFour channel was closed down and relaunched as Film4 on the Freeview digital terrestrial television platform. Press coverage described the move as a democratising process that would provide viewers with ready access to a formerly rarefied type of television content. For example, it was suggested in the *Independent*, 9 February 2006, that the UK's first free film channel would 'pose a fresh threat to Sky' in directly challenging one of its key programming areas in the context of a free broadcasting platform. Furthermore, the switch provided greater possibilities for Film4 to reach a larger audience share than would have been possible during its life as a niche subscription service.

This article will examine the shift in programming that took place during the life of the FilmFour channel, encompassing the launch of the subscription service in 1998, the Freeview switchover in 2006 and the first five years of the free Film4 service. Television listings samples will be used as the basis for investigating any changes in programming strategy during this period, providing a wealth of data that will be used to gauge the nationality, production period and genre of films screened on the channels between the years of 1998 and 2011. Through this analysis, links will be drawn between the evolution of the broadcaster's programming strategy and renewed attempts to fortify its public service remit and affirm its commitment to a 'culturally diverse' audience in the Freeview era.

The datasets

The quantitative datasets included in this article were extrapolated from television listings information held in the British Universities Film and Video Council's Television and Radio Index for Learning and Teaching (TRILT)[1] and Channel 4 Press Packs[2] online databases. I have produced four samples collected at different points across this thirteen-year period. The first covers FilmFour's launch week in November 1998. This data can be used to gauge the broadcaster's perceptions of the new subscription channel during this high-profile launch period. It also reveals the strategies used to attract viewers to the service and sheds some light on the perceived target audience(s) for the channel. The second sample was taken from November 2003, five years into the lifetime of the channel. An interregnum of this length was enforced because it reveals the changes in ethos that occurred in the years immediately following the channel's launch. It also represents a period of 'ordinary' scheduling, which is not attached to a major broadcasting event. In this respect, it provides a useful counterpoint to the launch week's schedule, a moment which would have been subject to intense public scrutiny and press coverage. The third sample was collected for the period commencing 17 July 2006 and focuses on the days immediately leading up to and following FilmFour's relaunch as the Freeview service Film4. Much like the subscription channel's launch period, the 2006 relaunch schedule reveals the broadcaster's intentions regarding how the Freeview service would be rolled out during subsequent months. Finally, a sample from 17 July 2011 is used again to impose a five-year gap between samples, allowing an interval from which to judge changes in ethos that occurred following the channel's relaunch.

Spanning an evolutionary period during which FilmFour became Film4, the 2006 sample has an unusual status. Although the switch from subscription to Freeview happened within a matter of days, the broadcaster had to develop a new brand identity while also making effective use of an existing library of film acquisitions. As such, it does not necessarily provide an accurate indication of Film4's identity and programming ethos. Instead, the inclusion of a final sample from 2011 provides a clearer picture of the acquisitions and scheduling strategies that have shaped Film4 in recent years. This sample covers a period of 'ordinary' scheduling, as distinct from any seasonal or institutional broadcasting events, and so it can be argued this provides a more typical indication of the kinds of films broadcast during a standard week on Film4.

With the exception of the third sample, which covers the longer transition from the subscription to Freeview service, each dataset includes an entire week of programming for the channel. The decision was made to cover a week's content in each sample because this reveals the patterns and shifts in programming that typically occur at specific times of day across a regular period. However, each sample varies in size due to several alterations in broadcasting hours that took place between 1998 and 2011. Because of this variation in sample size, data analysis will focus on the percentage of different types of film screened during each period rather than the number broadcast within any given sample. This should allow for a more accurate assessment of any shifts in programming that might have taken place. Analysis of the three datasets reveals the national origin (Table 1), production period (Table 2) and genre (Table 3) of films screened during each of the four collated sample periods. In the following section each of these variables will be interrogated and reviewed, together with developments in programming policy.

Nationality

One of the key areas to be analysed in this article is the range of national cinemas that have been represented on the subscription and Freeview channels throughout their different broadcasting periods. Perhaps unsurprisingly, English language features have constituted a substantial percentage of the films screened throughout this thirteen-year period. During the launch week in 1998, for instance, eighteen (38 per cent) of the films screened were of American production origin and ten (21 per cent) were British. In addition, three British and American co-productions were broadcast, and fourteen of the films screened were foreign-language productions originating from countries such as Italy, France, Japan, Mexico, Denmark and Spain (30 per cent). It can be concluded that the breadth of national cinemas represented during the launch week revealed the channel's

Table 1. Nationality of films

Year in which films were broadcast	1998	2003	2006	2011	Total
American	18	36	30	31	115
Australian	1		2		3
Belgian	1		1		2
British	10	6	14	23	53
Canadian		1	1		2
Cantonese			4	1	5
Chinese	1				1
Danish	1	2	1		4
French	5		5		10
German		2			2
Hungarian				1	1
Italian	1	3	1		5
Japanese	3	1		2	6
Mexican	1				1
Norwegian				1	1
Senegalese			1		1
Spanish	1		1		2
Swedish			1	1	2
American/British	3	2	2	7	14
American/German				2	2
British/French				1	1
British/French/German/Indian				1	1
Danish/French/German/ Polish/Swedish/Swiss		1			1
Dutch/British/French	1				1
French/Italian			2		2
Total	47	54	66	71	238

Table 2. Production period

Year in which films were broadcast	1998	2003	2006	2011	Total
1930s	2	1	7		10
1940s			6	5	11
1950s	2	2	3	16	23
1960s	5	7	4	5	21
1970s	3	6	4	4	17
1980s	9	14	3	4	30
1990s	26	18	11	3	58
2000s		6	28	34	68
Total	47	54	66	71	238

Table 3. Film genre

Year in which films were broadcast	1998	2003	2006	2011	Total
Animated drama			1	2	3
Comedy	10	5	14	18	47
Comedy/drama	5	3	4		12
Documentary	1		2		3
Drama	26	31	35	37	129
Drama/documentary	1				1
Family comedy				2	2
Fantasy		3		3	6
Horror	2	6	5	1	14
Horror/science fiction		3			3
Musical		1			1
Science fiction	2	1	5		8
Superhero/fantasy/action				2	2
Western		1		6	7
Total	47	54	66	71	238

initial commitment to international film cultures extending beyond the production borders of America and the United Kingdom.

The first night's broadcast, which was simulcast on both Channel 4 and FilmFour, commenced with screenings of contemporary American independent films *What's Eating Gilbert Grape?* (1993) and *The Usual Suspects* (1995). The choice of recently released American films made sound commercial sense within the high-profile context of the launch. Screened during peak viewing hours on Sunday, 1 November, these films offered a tantalising sample of what the new subscription channel had to offer. These features were followed later in the evening by Peter Greenaway's *The Pillow Book* (1995), which had received Channel 4 funding, and the Italian film *Caro Diario* (1994), which was screened during the early hours of the following morning. Table 1 reveals that a similar pattern continued throughout the first week on air, with a fairly even mix of American, British and foreign-language films. While foreign-language features were sometimes screened late at night or during the early hours of the morning, this was not always the case. Indeed, the Japanese period drama *Yojimbo* (1961) and French New Wave film *À bout de souffle* (*Breathless*) (1960) were screened on Thursday, 3 November, at 6 p.m. and 8 p.m. respectively. Scheduling international cinema during peak viewing hours reinforced the channel's commitment to this area of film programming. Furthermore, the inclusion of Japanese and French art-house films alongside other well respected foreign-language offerings revealed FilmFour's alignment with traditional cineaste culture. However, the channel also included playful schlock offerings such as the 1992 Japanese film *Godzilla vs Mothra*, which was screened in a 6 p.m. slot during the first week. Films of this sort alluded to the increasingly diverse tastes of film fans during the 1990s and the new credibility of 'guilty pleasure' and cult films.

Seven of the films screened on FilmFour during this 2003 period were foreign-language features produced between 1963 and 2000. The following films belong to this category: *The Princess and the Warrior* (2000), *Run Lola Run* (1999), *8½* (1963), *Brother* (2000), *Terror at the Opera* (1987), *Babette's Feast* (1987) and *Suspiria* (1976). Constituting 13 per cent of the total number of films in this sample, these productions were all screened on the channel after 10 p.m. Indeed, the majority of these titles were placed in slots commencing after midnight. While many of these films were not suitable for exhibition before the 9 p.m. watershed, their post-midnight scheduling also sheds some light on FilmFour's relationship with non-English language purchases at this time. Although such films were publicised widely in the promotional material used initially to stimulate interest in the channel, the decision to purchase features that could be broadcast only at the periphery of the schedule closed down possibilities for introducing foreign-language films into peak-time programming.

Table 1 reveals that films produced outside of the UK and America remained a significant feature of the Film4 schedule following the Freeview relaunch in 2006. Of the films screened during this sample period, fifteen were foreign-language, amounting to 23 per cent of the total features screened between 17 and 31 July. As suggested earlier, the initial Film4 schedule would have been informed by the broadcaster's existing library of films, many of which were purchased for transmission on the subscription channel. As such, this early schedule sample cannot be regarded as characteristic of Film4's programming in subsequent years. Rather, July 2006 represented a transitional period, with the sample revealing the broadcaster's initial attempts to distinguish between the characters of the subscription and Freeview channels. The film programming for this week provided a bridge between the two services, signalling the shift in content that was due to take place following the launch of Film4.

When the Freeview service was introduced on Sunday, 23 July, the selection of films provided an indication of the ethos that would inform the new channel. The first evening's broadcasts included screenings of *Lost in Translation* (2003) at 9 p.m., *Sexy Beast* (2000) at 11 p.m. and *Infernal Affairs* (2002) at 2:30 a.m. *Lost in Translation* is an American independent film that proved to be a significant crossover hit following its release – arguably due to the star status of its lead actor Bill Murray and the family connections of its director Sophia Coppola. This indiewood offering had a cultural prestige that reinforced the subscription channel's status as a 'quality' channel, while also being an accessible film that could appeal to a range of audiences. Although more of a cult hit, *Sexy Beast* is a well-respected British feature that received Channel 4 funding. The inclusion of this production reinforced Film4's continued commitment to the exhibition of recently produced British features. And finally, the Hong Kong crime film *Infernal Affairs* revealed the new channel's intended support for foreign-language cinema. However, it should be noted that this film is a relatively accessible thriller that has the potential to appeal to a mainstream television audience. It was also placed at the periphery of the schedule in a late-night slot that would typically command lesser viewing figures than it would in peak time. As the final scheduling sample will show, this pattern set the tone for subsequent years on the channel, when different segments would be given over to Hollywood, American and British independent film, and to foreign-language features. Although each area of programming would retain a sense of visibility on the channel, different categories of film were carefully compartmentalised within the schedule according to their intended audiences and perceived ratings status.

By 2011 Film4's broadcasting hours had been extended, with film screenings commencing at 11 a.m. rather than 3 p.m. as had previously been the case. As such, the channel required a greater number of purchased films to fill the schedule on a weekly basis. Table 1 shows that the number of features produced outside of the UK and America that were broadcast on the channel had significantly decreased by this point even though the total number of films screened on a weekly basis had increased significantly. For the selected sample period only seven of the 71 films screened were foreign-language, constituting a mere 10 per cent of the total number of features shown. Apart from family-friendly animated films such as *The Cat Returns* (2002) and *Kiki's Delivery Service* (1989), these were all screened in late-night slots outside the channel's peak viewing hours. These findings highlight the necessity of intersecting the nationality of films broadcast with data relating to their genre and production period. The age and genre of foreign-language films shown on the subscription and Freeview channels informed the scheduling strategies employed in their exhibition. There is a particularly strong correlation between the nationality and genre of films that have been exhibited by the broadcaster which will be explored in greater detail during the final section of this article.

Production period

For the purposes of this study, 'recent' films will be classed as those that were produced during the ten years preceding each sample period.[3] For instance, in the case of the 2011 sample, the category of recent films includes any features produced between the years 2001 and 2011. Through considering the age of films broadcast on the subscription and Freeview channels at different periods in their development, it will be possible to gauge the extent to which new releases have formed an important part of the channel's exhibition profile. Using the collected quantitative data enables calculation of the percentage of older films screened on the channel during each sample period. Close schedule analysis allows for contextualisation of this data and assessment of the strategies used to screen both old and new releases across a range of time slots.

When examining FilmFour's first week of scheduled content following the channel's launch, it becomes apparent that 27 of the films shown during this period were released in the ten years prior to November 1998. Allowing for the fact that some of these films were repeated several days after their initial screening, features produced during this ten-year period constituted 57 per cent of the channel's total output between 1 and 9 November. Recent releases formed an important part of the channel's early identity, filling much of the peak-time schedule. A number of these films were American independent productions featuring fashionable young stars such as Johnny Depp, Leonardo DiCaprio, Juliette Lewis, Catherine Keener, Matt Dillon, Joaquin Phoenix, Casey Affleck and Christian Slater. The inclusion of films featuring this particular brand of offbeat 1990s star represented an attempt to appeal to FilmFour's key ABC1 target demographic. Indeed, the author of the broadcaster's 1998 Annual Report acknowledged that Channel 4 successfully continued to appeal to both youth and upmarket adult audiences across much of its programming (Channel Four Television Corporation 1998: 32) and that FilmFour was designed to extend this relationship with 'Channel 4's core audience' (ibid.: 19). This appeal to young and/or upmarket audiences was also apparent in the choice of American cult directors such as Quentin Tarantino and the Coen brothers, whose films were screened during the first week of programming. Barbara Klinger has suggested that independent directors of this sort are particularly attractive to younger viewers, as they are the authors of 'outlaw texts' that are 'able to deliver either entertainment or aesthetic experience that exceeds what mainstream films can offer' (2006: 149).

Jessica Levick, the Rights and Sales Manager for Channel 4's library of films, has alluded to the role that critical acclaim can play in creating renewed interest in an actor's earlier production credits. In a recent interview she suggested that the respective Academy Award nominations received by Colin Firth and Daniel Day Lewis in 2011 and 2013 provided a platform through which their earlier appearances in Channel 4 films could be publicised.[4] As Levick implies, stars have their moments, informed by factors such as award wins and nominations. The dynamics informing star popularity are often transient and cannot be relied upon as enduring beyond a specific moment in time. As such, the age of films broadcast on FilmFour and Film4 can be assessed in relation to the star appeal of their leading performers. In the case of this early sample, stardom is not directly linked to Academy Award success or to other accolades bestowed by awarding bodies. Films such as *What's Eating Gilbert Grape?* (1993), *The Usual Suspects* (1995), *Fever Pitch* (1996), *Reservoir Dogs* (1992) and *Romeo is Bleeding* (1993) starred popular actors who had, by the end of the decade, come to characterise the zeitgeist of the 1990s. While Kevin Spacey had received an Oscar for his role in *The Usual Suspects*, he was the exception rather than the rule in this group of films. The stars showcased on Film4 during this period were known for their cult appeal, physical attractiveness and/or personalities rather than for their mainstream awards success. Although a star such as Leonardo DiCaprio was a popular performer at this time, following his casting in James Cameron's blockbuster *Titanic* (1997), he had yet to prove himself as a 'serious' actor, eligible for Academy Award nominations. Because these stars had not been canonised by Hollywood, their appropriation by Film4 reinforced the broadcaster's independent status. At this stage, the subscription channel represented an alternative to the mainstream, meaning that Oscar-nominated stars and films did not dominate the schedule.

Table 2 reveals that 20 (or 43 per cent) of the films screened during 1998 fall within the 'older' category, having been produced prior to 1988. Apart from the French film *Pépé le Moko* (1936), all of these older films had been released between 1955 and 1987. The oldest of these belonged to the French New Wave, revealing FilmFour's allegiance with cineaste culture and youthful cinematic rebellion, which was consistent with its support for the American independent cinema of the 1990s. Of the Channel 4 films screened during this sample period, 71 per cent were produced between 1988 and 1998. Evidently this was a period during which FilmFour's scheduling teams sought to remind viewers of the broadcaster's recent production history rather than of its theatrical/cinematic past. The increased publicity associated with the launch and the simulcast would provide opportunities for new audiences to gain an awareness of Channel 4's active role as a film funder.

For the purposes of the second sample, 'recent' films will be described as any which were released between 1993 and 2003. Of the films screened in 2003, eighteen were released during these years, representing 33 per cent of the total films screened during this week, while 36 of the films broadcast were released prior to 1993, representing 67 per cent of the total films screened during the sample period. These findings reveal that the screening of recent productions on the channel was less of a priority five years after FilmFour's launch than it had been during its first week on air. Arguably, newer films were used during the launch period as a means of enticing subscribers to sign up for the service. Indeed, when FilmFour was still largely an unknown quantity, marketing campaigns foregrounded the availability of up-to-the-minute content and recent independent releases that audiences may not have been able to access elsewhere.

While assessing the accumulated data for the 2003 sample, I found that films falling within the older category spanned a broad range of production periods, with the earliest having been released in 1937 and the most recent in 1992. Interestingly, the age of these films did not appear to have a significant bearing on where they were placed in the FilmFour schedule. For instance, although the 1937 feature *Lost Horizon* was screened at 3:50 a.m. on 6 November, *The Bad and the Beautiful* (1952) – released more than 50 years prior to the transmission date – was broadcast at 6 p.m. on 5 November. Older films were not ghettoised in FilmFour's late-night graveyard slots, as might have been expected, but appeared instead across a range of time periods according to their suitability and BBFC classification. While certain peak-time slots were given over to more commercial fare, such as the 1999 American teen film *Cruel Intentions*, this 8 p.m. to 10 p.m. segment of the schedule was also used to screen films with less obvious audience appeal, such as the 1965 MGM comedy *The Rounders*.

Significantly, the switch to Freeview heralded an upsurge in the overall percentage of older films appearing on the channel. During the transition to Freeview, the schedule increasingly featured classic

British and American films that had been released during the 1940s and 1950s. The 2006 sample includes titles such as *This Happy Breed* (1944), *Voyage to Italy* (1953), *The Way Ahead* (1944), *Double Indemnity* (1944), *The African Queen* (1951) and *Brief Encounter* (1945). As shown in previous samples, the 1940s and 1950s were decades whose films had remained largely absent from the subscription channel. Following the launch of the Freeview service, films that had been theatrically released during these decades were typically screened between 3 p.m. and 7 p.m.

The increasing prominence of older films within Film4's schedule during this period can be related to the broadcaster's reappraisal of its public service values during the latter half of the 2000s. In 2008 Channel 4 released a policy document entitled *Next on 4*, which sought to evaluate the broadcaster's ethos in relation to the shifting demands of multi-channel television and media convergence. Throughout the document there are attempts to address Channel 4's ostensibly conflicted status as public service broadcaster and commercial enterprise (Channel Four Television Corporation 2008: 63). The document concludes that in order to maintain its public service activities, Channel 4 needs to embrace commercial and remit programming in equal measure arguing that:

> While Channel 4's activities across all platforms will contribute to the delivery of our public purposes, not everything we do need be public service in nature. There has always been room for more commercial activities, whether programmes on Channel 4 that are purely populist, entertaining or commercial, or new commercial ventures that drive new income streams for the organisation. (Ibid.: 63)

The Film4 schedule provided a context in which this negotiation of the conflicting demands of public service and commercial activities could take place. As already discussed, the channel's broadcasting hours had been extended during the latter half of the 2000s to include daytime, afternoon and evening programming. The need to fill the expanded schedule allowed morning and early afternoon segments to become zones in which Hollywood and British films from the 1940s and 1950s could be viewed on a regular basis. Micro-identities were established within the Film4 schedule, whereby specific timeslots regularly featured the same types of film. This represents an extension of the practice of 'blocking' or 'stacking', whereby similar types of programme are placed alongside one another in order to retain viewers (Bellamy and Walker 1996: 75). The daytime screening of films produced prior to 1960 offered nostalgic viewing pleasures to an older audience of retired viewers more likely to watch television during the daytime. As such, following the launch of Freeview, Film4's perceived audience extended beyond the narrow 18–35 ABC1 core Channel 4 demographic originally targeted by the subscription service. Although not directly addressing sexual or ethnic minorities in a manner consistent with Channel 4's earlier public service ethos, this did nonetheless represent a step towards greater programming diversity for the channel.

As suggested in *Next on 4*, public service activities had to be offset by commercial programming choices in other areas of the schedule too. In the case of Film4, an increasingly populist strategy was applied to the scheduling of films within peak viewing zones. The 2011 sample shows that slots between the hours of 6 p.m. and 10:30 p.m. often showcased recent Hollywood productions that were likely to appeal to a mainstream audience. Titles scheduled in this segment included *Night at the Museum* (2006), *Crash* (2004), *Big Momma's House 2* (2006), *Fantastic Four: Rise of the Silver Surfer* (2007), *Iron Man* (2008), *S1m0ne* (2002), *The Happening* (2008), *Chocolat* (2000) and *Mission Impossible III* (2006). The variation between daytime and peak-time programming on the channel reveals the shift towards a complex scheduling and branding strategy that allows Film4 to successfully address a range of audiences. Film4 is no longer a channel devoted to a clearly definable demographic, unlike its sister channels More4 and E4, which address respectively upmarket ABC1 and 16–34-year-old viewers. Instead, it utilises a scheduling strategy that operates at a 'micro' level, whereby different periods of the day are devoted to specific types of content and audience demographics.

Genre

Due to the size of each of the programming samples, which include 238 films in total, it has been necessary to assign fairly broad genre classifications to each feature referenced. Although familiar with a number of the films screened on the subscription and Freeview channels during these periods, I have had to use online databases such as IMDb as a means of assigning classifications to those that I have not personally viewed. While this method had its limitations, there were also benefits to using IMDb, which provided a useful insight into how certain films have widely been perceived in genre terms. Indeed, genre is open to interpretation, and multiple taxonomic boundaries are liable to overlap in individual films. As such, it has been necessary to avoid complex cross-genre classifications, opting instead for expansive categories such as 'drama', 'comedy', 'horror' and 'science fiction' in my quantitative survey. The genre nuances and complex identities of individual films are acknowledged in my subsequent analysis of each of the four samples, although the breadth of data has necessitated an empirical rather than an in-depth case study approach.

When FilmFour first launched in 1998, the channel's foremost genre was drama. Of the films listed in Table 3, 26 can be categorised as dramas, constituting 55 per cent of the total films broadcast during this period. Although 21 per cent of the films screened during the FilmFour launch week can be classified as comedies, the majority of these features fall within the category of black comedy, being defined as such because thematically they are more sinister than mainstream comedy films. There are also a number of films that straddle the generic divide between comedy and drama, and these constitute 11 per cent of scheduled content. Other genres represented in this sample include horror, science fiction, documentary and documentary drama, which collectively constitute 13 per cent of the sample schedule. This configuration and the pervasiveness of films aimed at adult, rather than family, audiences suggested a seriousness of tone on the part of the new channel, which promised in its marketing material to present 'cult classics and underrated films' without accepting any 'compromises'.[5]

This ethos continued to inform programming during subsequent years, as drama remained the prevalent film genre represented throughout the schedule. Nevertheless, Table 3 does reveal an increase in genre diversity, with a noticeable surge in the number of horror films broadcast on the channel in 2003, including *The Evil Dead* (1983), *Re-Animator* (1985), *The Bride of Re-Animator* (1990), *Terror at the Opera* (1987), *Blood Feast* (1963) and *Two Thousand Maniacs* (1964). The screening of these 'extreme' horror films can be seen as a logical extension of FilmFour's commitment to cult films aimed at an adult audience. Other genres represented in the 2003 sample include a selection of science fiction and fantasy productions, one western and one musical feature.

The spread of genres represented within Table 3 also intersects with data relating to national cinema coverage. When the character of individual films included in the 2003 sample is assessed, it becomes apparent that there is a distinct lack of genre diversity in the area of the foreign-language film. Foreign-language offerings included the violent Japanese crime drama *Brother* and the Italian horror films *Suspiria* and *Terror at the Opera*. As already suggested, foreign-language features were screened predominantly late at night on the subscription channel. This was largely because the foreign-language films included in the 2003 schedule had been assigned a BBFC classification that made them unsuitable for pre-watershed broadcasting. The channel's affiliation with counter-cultural and peripheral cinema meant that a horror film such as *Suspiria* made much more sense as a FilmFour foreign-language acquisition than – for instance – a period saga such as *Jean de Florette* (1986). Indeed, while historical dramas usually belong in the daytime or early evening segments of a channel's programming and are designed to appeal to a range of audience demographics, horror films are assigned typically to late-night slots. Thus, in predominantly supporting genres of foreign-language film aimed at an adult audience, FilmFour's purchasers and schedulers allowed late-night and early-morning segments of the schedule to become designated foreign cinema zones.

It was not until the Freeview relaunch that comic genres emerged as a significant category within the Film4 schedule. From 2006 onwards, comedy films started to appear regularly within the channel's daytime programming zones. This increased inclusion of the genre can be related to the screening of 1940s and 1950s features in daytime segments of the schedule during the 2006–11 period. Many of these classical Hollywood and British films are family-friendly comedies, or comedy dramas, suitable for transmission prior to the watershed. Although targeting an older viewer demographic, the scheduling of these films also opened up the possibility for a younger audience engaged in inter-generational viewing activities as part of a family group.

The extension of daytime programming hours to attract broader audience demographics was accompanied by the emergence of another film category on the channel. Following the launch of the Freeview service, the broadcaster increasingly screened family and teen-oriented features such as *Night at the Museum, The Cat Returns, Stardust* (2007), *Kiki's Delivery Service* and *Angus, Thongs and Perfect Snogging* (2008). On a practical level these films filled the expanded daytime schedule, providing acceptable, ratings-friendly alternatives to features produced during the 1940s and 1950s. Furthermore, they reached out to an audience of children and young teens and thus targeted a group that had previously fallen outside of the channel's programming remit. The 2011 sample also included the popular superhero movies *Fantastic Four: Rise of the Silver Surfer* (2007) and *Iron Man* (2008) in peak viewing slots, reflecting both the rise of this genre at the box office during the latter half of the 2000s and the genre's ability to achieve crossover success with mainstream, cult and teen audiences.

When examining the 2011 sample, it is apparent that a number of the films broadcast in evening viewing slots during this period were comedies. Although black comedies and comedy dramas have continued to appear on the Freeview channel in recent years, it now also regularly screens frat pack and gross-out American movies featuring actors such as Ben Stiller, Owen Wilson, Will Ferrell and Vince Vaughan. The inclusion of titles such as *Without a Paddle* (2004) and *Stuck on You* (2003) in the 2011 sample reflects the increasing popular appeal of this type of film production to British audiences. Scheduled respectively at 11:10 p.m. and 11:20 p.m., they include adult humour and language that would not typically be deemed suitable for exhibition prior to the watershed. Once again, these are films that are capable of attracting a range of audiences, including 16–34-year-old viewers, comedy fans and cult film enthusiasts. Their inclusion in the schedule reinforces the move away from the subscription channel's brand identity as a 'serious' film channel, predominantly screening feature-length dramas. This programming shift has allowed Film4's evening viewing slots to become branded as playful zones with populist credentials.

Conclusion

Close analysis of scheduling data reveals distinctive programming patterns that have characterised Channel 4's subscription and Freeview film channels during key periods in their shared history. The birth of the Freeview service provided an opportunity for Channel 4 to reframe its relationship with film in an evolving multi-channel environment. While the FilmFour subscription channel targeted a niche audience of 'high-brow' film fans and cineastes, Film4 currently uses a 'blocking' technique to create a compartmentalised schedule targeting different audience demographics at segmented intervals throughout each day. This diversity of content can be attributed partially to the increased commercial pressures brought about by the launch of Freeview. The extension of Film4's broadcasting hours created the need for a greater volume of content, including a distinct quota appealing to an audience of daytime television viewers. This has resulted in the screening of a larger number of films on the channel which were produced prior to 1960. Through filling morning and afternoon slots with family-friendly films produced during the 1940s and 1950s, the channel targets a varied daytime audience, which includes an older viewing demographic.

Increased broadcasting hours have also engendered a shift in genre emphasis. The rebranded Film4 channel now provides a space in which the broadcaster can screen films aimed at an audience of children and young teens previously not included in the channel's programming ethos. This has resulted in the scheduling of animated dramas, family comedies and superhero movies, all of which had been absent from earlier programming samples. However, this opening up of genre representation in certain areas has been accompanied by a diminishing representation in others. While horror and science fiction had been mainstays of the subscription service, together constituting 19 per cent of films screened during the 2003 sample period, in 2011 they represented only 1 per cent of all films sampled. This was accompanied by a decrease in foreign-language programming, much of which had belonged to the horror genre and accordingly had been screened after the watershed for an audience of adult viewers. As the volume of foreign-language features diminished, evening slots increasingly featured more commercially viable Hollywood and British films.

Although the multi-channel landscape has undeniably given rise to greater competition for advertising revenue in the television sector, it has also resulted in a greater diversity of content available to viewers at no cost other than that of the licence fee. As revealed by *Next on 4*, the evolving commercial environment prompted Channel 4 to reappraise its role as a public service broadcaster. In the case of Film4 this resulted in the development of a micro schedule whereby different periods of the day were opened up to viewing demographics that had not been targeted by the earlier subscription channel. Specific times of the day now include clearly defined genres, national cinemas and periods of film that will be recognisable to regular Film4 viewers. Through extending its remit beyond that of its original upmarket adult audience, the channel now actively addresses a range of viewing demographics and attempts to reflect the tastes and interests of a culturally diverse television audience.

Acknowledgements
I would like to thank Channel 4 for providing access to their archives; Rosie Gleeson and Evike Galajda were particularly generous with their time and expertise. I would also like to thank Jessica Levick for her helpful interview.

Notes
1. TRILT can be accessed via < http://bufvc.ac.uk/tvandradio/trilt/ > .
2. The Channel 4 Press Packs can be accessed via < http://bufvc.ac.uk/tvandradio/c4pp > .
3. The following calculations show the percentage of 'recent' films screened during each sample period:

   - 1998 sample: 1988 onwards (produced during previous ten years): 27 films, 57 per cent of all films shown;
   - 2003 sample: 1993 onwards (produced during the previous ten years): 18 films, 33 per cent of all films shown;
   - 2006 sample: 1996 onwards (produced during the previous ten years): 34 films, 52 per cent of all films shown;
   - 2011 sample: 2001 onwards (produced during the previous ten years): 33 films 46 per cent of all films shown.

4. Interview with the author, 11 January 2013.
5. Pull-out glossy advertisements for the FilmFour channel that appeared in *The Times Magazine*, 27 March 1999, Box: 6/PP/265/2, File: 'FilmFour 98, File 2 of 2', Channel 4 Archive Collections.

References

Bellamy, R. V. and Walker, James R. (1996), *Television and the Remote Control: Grazing on a Vast Wasteland*, New York: Guilford Press.

Channel Four Television Corporation (1998), *Channel Four Television Corporation Report and Financial Statements 1998*, London: Channel Four Television Corporation.

Channel Four Television Corporation (2004), *Channel Four Television Corporation Report and Financial Statements 2004*, London: Channel Four Television Corporation.

Channel Four Television Corporation (2008), *Next on 4*, London: Channel Four Television Corporation.

Communications Act 2003 (2003), London: TSO, available at: < http://www.legislation.gov.uk/ukpga/2003/21/pdfs/ukpga_20030021_en.pdf > (accessed 20 August 2013).

Klinger, B. (2006), *Beyond the Multiplex: Cinema, New Technologies and the Home*, Berkeley, CA: University of California Press.

Rachael Keene is a doctoral candidate at the University of Portsmouth. Her PhD thesis, 'Channel 4 Television: Film Policy and Programming, 1982–2011' – part of the AHRC project 'Channel 4 and British Film Culture' – assesses Channel 4's contribution to British film culture, as both a commissioner and an exhibitor of film and film-related programming. Her research focuses on the impact that technological and institutional developments have upon broadcasting strategy.

The Four Heads of Film4

Justin Smith and Laura Mayne

Introduction

There have been four key figures responsible for Channel 4's film production activities since the Channel's inception in 1982. David Rose, David Aukin, Paul Webster and Tessa Ross have each ensured that Channel 4 retains its key commitment to promoting British film culture, as envisioned by its first chief executive Jeremy Isaacs. They have presided over film and drama through changes within the corporate structure and financing of the Channel, through deregulation of the television industry and the expansion of the independent production sector, through the growth of the digital economy and multi-channel television, and through changes in the funding landscape and the fortunes of the UK film industry. As vital contributors to the film culture they have each expressed their own individual passion for and commitment to British film, have championed establish film-makers and nurtured new talent, and have worked tirelessly to advance British film on the world stage and to broaden its domestic audience base. Occupying a unique position at the interface of the television and film industries, and between the cultural patronage of public service broadcasting and international co-production finance, they share a rare skill above all: an eye for a good script.

Justin Smith

David Rose

David Rose was Senior Commissioning Editor (Fiction) at Channel 4, 1981–9.

Journal of British Cinema and Television 11.4 (2014): 517–551
Edinburgh University Press
DOI: 10.3366/jbctv.2014.0232
© *Journal of British Cinema and Television*
www.euppublishing.com/jbctv

Justin Smith and Laura Mayne

Interviewer: Justin Smith
Interview: 27 May 2010

JS: *Is it true to say that what Channel 4 achieved, and what British television ultimately achieved, was following a model of a relationship between film and television that had existed in Europe, certainly in Germany and Italy, for some years beforehand?*

DR: Yes. I went to Germany with Jeremy[1] two days before I joined Channel 4 in 1981, which was 18 months before going on air.[2] Two nights – we went to Munich, where a woman he knew, I didn't know then but I know very well now, Renee Goddard,[3] had fixed up a meeting of television and film producers. And Jeremy did his little spiel. And that night we went to the opera and saw *Don Giovanni*. And then we went on to ZDF,[4] who were the real model for *us* anyway, who were doing precisely what Jeremy picked up – supporting films which could be released in the cinema before being screened on television. We had a meeting at ZDF and then went to Cologne – did the same thing again there, and went to the opera again!

JS: *To what extent did your experience at Pebble Mill as Head of English Regions Drama[5] prepare you for what was an unknown quantity at the new Channel 4?*

DR: I found it a smooth transition. It seemed to me, I said so at the time, that it was pretty well exactly what I was doing in Pebble Mill.

JS: *You started off with £6 million didn't you? Something like that?*

DR: £6 million and hoping to realise 20 features. I was blissfully in a position where there was so much support from Colin Leventhal,[6] on the lawyer's side, and Sara Geater,[7] on the finance side. Sara dealt with the films being over-budget, and schedules, and if there were problems that were reflected editorially, she would come to us and get our view. If we were concerned about this that or the other we would go to her and say 'we must ensure we have time to do that, and we think that's an important aspect of the film, or whatever'. You see it was all remarkably smooth I must say. And there were so many independents. The independent sector had hardly existed, certainly for feature films, before Channel 4.

JS: *And did the scripts come in thick and fast?*

DR: There must have been, for every project we gave a green light to, another five we didn't, at least. But Walter Donohue[8] was the one chap I invited to be my assistant. And there was Karin Bamborough,[9] who was working at the channel for Michael Kustow, who was the Commissioning Editor for the Arts.[10] He knew Karin Bamborough who worked in the literary department of the National Theatre, and he said would she look at the whole of the country and Europe, and give him a sort of picture of what was going on when he finally arrived at the channel. And she did that, but she spent more time in the office reading our scripts! And eventually Jeremy said, 'Look, she should be with you as well.' So she came on board as well.

JS: *Walter and Karin both had literary backgrounds rather than film or television then?*

DR: It's true that on reflection the people I encouraged to join television – like Peter Ansorge, Michael Wearing, Tara Prem, Barry Hanson[11] – none of them had ever worked with the screen before. And I was rather pleased to think they didn't have any baggage in that respect. But particularly they all in their own way knew writing things was the principle.

JS: *And you, the three of you obviously had an enormous number of scripts to get through, but presumably also you were responsible to some extent for seeing how the money was spent on projects that you green-lit?*

DR: Yes, I had to go to the finance meetings, and was questioned on things that arose. I was able to have the clout that was necessary. It was the editorial side of things that mattered in terms of balancing where the money should go. But you were asking earlier about the policy and so forth? We never talked about it! We took it for granted that it was a question of a good script, and it was also taken as read when you hired someone they were of a *like* mind, not too similar, but you could have a view that we all shared somehow. It was unspoken really. I think that was somehow to do with the people one worked with. Jeremy trusted me. I think he liked a lot of what he saw coming out of Birmingham, so it was understood: we knew we were going for variety. I was rather anxious that we were going to have a fair representation of the political scene in the country, and it seemed that in the 1980s it was even more difficult than in the 1970s to get writers' attention in that direction.

When you look at it there were very few things like *The Ploughman's Lunch* (1983). But not that I would wish to be too direct about any political situation! Ken Loach gets a bit heavy at times in that direction.

JS: *There was certainly an emphasis on the contemporary drama, but nonetheless a number of period costume films were also made.*

DR: Some of our best. *A Month in the Country* (1987). A fabulous film. And the Scottish one with the Italian prisoners of war: *Another Time, Another Place* (1983), directed by Michael Radford. That has always been one of my favourites. I think partly because it did what we were trying to do in Birmingham, showing a particular regional sense of place and time.

JS: *Was that something you were looking for, particularly, in a good script?*

DR: Always there was the sense of, 'Was it visual?' Some people say they can't visualise when they read a script. And I think some of us can. You can see it in your own way, and I don't think I ever got to the end of a script and said, 'Well that's a bloody good script but it's not *visual* enough.' One just hopes always that it will be made by a director, and particularly a cinematographer, who has a good visual eye and that the script offers them the opportunity to *do* that.

JS: *Perhaps the film that most people associate with Film on Four in the 1980s is* My Beautiful Laundrette *(1985). Can you say something about how that came into being?*

DR: That film of course started *here*, with my wife. Karin Bamborough said, 'I'm having lunch with Hanif Kureishi.' Just about to leave Charlotte Street. I said, 'Well who's he? I've not heard of him.' She said, 'Well he writes plays and puts them on in pubs.' She came back and said, 'I think we should commission him, he's got a good idea.' That was in May, and so we commissioned him and Karin worked on the script with him a bit and in July he cycled round and shoved it through Stephen Frears' door. And it was Stephen of course who said, 'Can we have a meeting, I want to direct this?' And he recommended the production company, Working Title, and Sarah Radclyffe.[12] It was their first feature. So we had a meeting and happily I think at that moment somebody's film had gone down and so we had £650,000 which we said, 'is yours', you know. It was just like that. And it was completed by March. I mean there's no merit in making a film quickly really, but it all happened within a very short space of time and then of course it took off and went to Edinburgh. But it was very refreshing.

JS: *And shot originally on 16mm I believe?*

DR: Super 16mm I think. I remember seeing it just off Broadway in New York, and they'd tried to make it looked wider than it was. Stephen was quite sure it would never travel south of the river here! He said, 'This is a telly film', but it shows how he got it wrong!

JS: *That distinction is a fascinating one, and one that I think becomes increasingly blurred with the Films on Four. But precisely what it did was to change our conceptions about what television drama is, and our preconceptions about British cinema. Another aspect of the diversity of the films you supported was your involvement in European cinema too.*

DR: We did a few early foreign films, subtitled. I think we called it 'Film Four International'. And the audience was building you know, even on that. And now no one trusts it. They stick it out at midnight. It's a great shame.

JS: *Not only were you buying in overseas films for broadcast but also, increasingly, began to commission work or at least put some money into overseas projects.*

DR: We didn't acquire things in my department. One or two recommendations I made: certainly *In the White City* (*Dans La Ville Blanche*) (1983). I don't know whether we called that a Film on Four. Alain Tanner. Wonderful film. With Bruno Ganz. Set in Lisbon. I recommended that when I saw it in Cannes I think. But the international scene: certainly Wim Wenders, we had a good relationship with him [JS: *Paris, Texas* (1984)]. Yes, he always said we put the first brick in the floor – the first finance into that. Who did that road movie – Chris Petit? [JS: *Radio On* (1980)]. *Radio On*. And then he wanted to do a film, *Flight to Paris*. And he was talking to Wim about it, and Wim said 'Yes – perhaps you'll back my film if I help you with that, but you'll have to call it *Flight to Berlin*'! I didn't enjoy the film that came out very much. Then I was in Sicily, at some conference, and the Head of the Swedish Film Institute, a woman, came up to me and said, 'I'm going to produce and put a third of the budget into Tarkovsky's *The Sacrifice* (1986), will you make a contribution?' And I said 'Yes' straight away. And there was a woman at that conference, who, at the end of the evening we'd been drinking and so forth, and she came up and said, 'Mr Rose – you don't really know who I am, do you? I'm Agnes Varda.' 'Of course I know.' She said, 'Right, breakfast in the morning.' And she gave me a little lesson about who she was. She needed some finishing money for that film that we called *Vagabonds (Vagabonde)* (1985) with that wonderful French actress Sandrine Bonnaire. And Theo Angelopoulos [JS: Yes. *Voyage to Cythera* (1984)]. That's right. He refused to speak English. His wife seemed to do all the interpretation. The leading actor was ill in that, and the whole thing had to be completed nine months later.

JS: *The international aspect appears to have been a growing trend. Were you aware of that, that you'd started off funding the independent sector in British film production and you were increasingly, as Channel 4's reputation for feature film grew, making a mark in European art cinema?*

DR: It grew as an initiative – we found we were interested in more and more. They were interested in ZDF and a channel like ours, who would support them. They were looking for money I suppose. Again, it wasn't something we sat down and had a meeting about and decided we should do more of them. It was just the way it went – it grew on its own. And there's no doubt that it spread the word about a new channel in Britain – Channel 4 Television. Around the world. Because it was a popular channel at all these film festivals. If anything we really acted as an advertisement for the new channel.

JS: *To bring things full circle, it was fitting then, that the work that you had pioneered at Channel 4 was recognised at Cannes in the presentation of the Roberto Rossellini Award for Services to Cinema.*

DR: That was really the culmination [of my career]. That brought it all together for me. At last they [the cinema and television industries] were recognising one another formally.

David Aukin

David Aukin was Head of Film and Drama at Channel 4, 1990–8.

Interviewer: Justin Smith
Interview: 18 November 2013

JS: *As I understand it there was actually something of a hiatus between David Rose retiring and your appointment; there's a sense in which that was the end* *of an era: Film Four Mark 1. Did you feel that you were inheriting a mantle and a set of expectations, or did the brief that Liz Forgan[13] give you allow you to make the role your own and to start again as it were?*

DA: Well, first of all I wasn't just appointed as Head of Film Four, I was head of all Drama on the Channel, and it was certainly made very clear to me by Michael [Grade][14] at the interview I had with him prior to taking up the post that he wouldn't object if I came to him and said I wanted to close down Film Four, that it had fulfilled its role in the last eight years or whatever it was, and it was fine if I wanted to focus entirely on television drama, that would have his support. And I said, 'Well, let me test the waters' as it were, and six months later I said to him, 'I don't think there is anything wrong with Film Four; I think there's a lot of talent out there and it's never been more needed than it is now and I think we can make something of it.' And so the decision was made, for the moment anyway, to continue. There was always the Sword of Damocles hanging over its head in those early days: if it didn't deliver why continue?

JS: *You came to Channel 4 with a background in theatre. How did your prior experience prepare you for the job of as Head of Film4?*

DA: Well, it was a question I consistently put to Liz Forgan and Michael Grade! And they made it very clear their approach (and it wasn't just to film or drama, it was across the board) was not to have specialists as such but to have people whose judgement and tastes they trusted to take responsibility for whatever discipline they were engaged for, and they had obviously seen my track record in theatre and just thought well here's someone who can apply that across to another discipline, namely film and TV. And of course it was a gamble and I think that was in a period when the channel, and the whole landscape of television, was in a very different place from where it is today. It wasn't as centralised in those days as it is today and you were on a four-year contract and if you didn't deliver they didn't renew it, it's as simple as that.

JS: *I was interested in what you said about having the opportunity to test the water. What was it that convinced you that Film Four was worth going on with then?*

DA: It was meeting the film-makers and the ideas that came through, like Neil Jordan and Mike Leigh and a host of others, and I just felt there was a real hunger out there for money to make the films they were all desperate to make, and there wasn't a lot of money to be got elsewhere. I thought the channel had a really important role to play.

JS: *And how did you organise your team around you, because again that was a kind of new-look scene compared with the people David Rose had around him. There was a kind of general sense of transition to a new era, wasn't there?*

DA: Yes. I mean, David obviously had a much wider knowledge of cinema and television on a practical basis than I could bring to the job, but the whole point was that I perceived that my job wasn't to get involved in how films were made, it was in choosing the people and the projects and having trust and belief in them. And one area where we did get very involved was in script and in that regard I realised, I felt very quickly, very early on, that I needed a very good script editor to work with me and alongside me. And I consulted a number of people and it was David Puttnam in fact who suggested I contact an American called Jack Lechner.[15] He was working at the time in Los Angeles and Jack agreed to come and join me which I think was quite a revelation. Again, if my appointment was shocking to the film industry Jack's was even worse: what was this American barbarian doing coming to fiddle around with our screenplays?! But of course Jack was a very smart man, *is* a very smart man, and I think film-makers soon grew to trust him and value him as much as I did.

JS: *One of your early projects was The Crying Game (1992). How did Jack Lechner work with Neil Jordan?*

DA: It was my second year probably. There is a timing issue with film, unlike TV drama which you can make relatively quickly from commissioning to being on screen. With film in those days not only did you have the time it took from commissioning to actually delivering, but then there was usually a two or three year bar on it being shown on television, because in those days people were terrified that the film audience would detract from the TV audience, which was a complete and total misconception. I think it is now understood that the exhibition in cinemas merely acts as a marketing tool for when it's shown on TV. The more successful it is in cinema the bigger the audience. But we didn't know that in those days, people didn't understand it. So there was this big time lag between the commissioning and when *The Crying Game* came out in 1992. And I felt that the script for *The Crying Game* wasn't quite knitting together, and so it was great that Jack was there to go over to Dublin and sit with Neil and talk it through.

JS: *I understand from Stephen Woolley*[16] *that there was quite a creative struggle around that film?*

DA: Well, it was only because there was a sense in which it was slightly broken-backed, in that it started with the kidnapping of a British soldier and developed into this other story, and how do you unify these two strands to make any unity of it all? And it's a common problem with many films. And I think as a result of our probings Neil came up with what I thought was a brilliant solution which really worked. But you know they did the work, we just asked the questions!

JS: *You developed a reputation, expressed in one or two things you wrote, for wanting to move away from the heritage film. The literary adaptation had been, of course, hugely popular and successful, not just to Channel 4 but elsewhere. But it seemed that you were keener on more genre-based kinds of project, and* The Crying Game, *as a political thriller, works brilliantly in that regard. Is that a fair judgement?*

DA: Yes. I don't think it was unique to me and, I think David Rose had a not dissimilar agenda and did some extraordinary contemporary films but also some adaptations that I was very proud for us to be involved with like Merchant/Ivory's *Howards End* (1992), which I thought was a terrific movie. But yes, in my more pretentious mode I would say I would like to think that at the end of my time the films I commissioned provide a snapshot of Britain in the 1990s, and not Britain in the 1890s!

JS: *Of course* Film on Four *in the early 1990s quickly arrived at its tenth anniversary and there was a sense perhaps of beginning to look back over its history. How significant was it, in the way that you were thinking about new projects, that you had this strand to fill, because that television broadcast strand petered out, didn't it?*

DA: Yes, it was absolutely a rejigging of the perception of how a TV schedule works and where there would be literally seasons of *Film on Four* twice a year, we would have to select thirty films from the previous year – actually it was from the previous three years because we were waiting for the current films to get released – and we had to make up these seasons. And over the period I was at the channel this dependence on seasons was gradually and unceremoniously dropped, and they just realised the way to schedule a film was the best place for the film to go rather than within a particular slot, at, say, 9 o'clock on a Thursday.

JS: *And particularly since, unlike other regular broadcast slots, you had relatively little control over what was available to fill it at any one time?*

DA: Certainly the first couple of years with the hiatus between myself and David there was that distinct feeling of the cupboard being if not bare at least not being full of goodies.

JS: *And what was your relationship with Michael Grade like because it was known that, unlike Jeremy Isaacs, his predecessor, Grade was emphatically a television man and not terribly interested in film. I gather that* Shallow Grave *(1994), in particular, was a film he wasn't terribly keen on?*

DA: When he first saw the film he really did react very strongly against it and he didn't feel it was a film he could even transmit on television. So you then fast-forward six months and the film is a huge success at the British box office and was winning awards all over the world and yes, it is a film that skipped generations and it was a film that young people really warmed to and older people tended not to. But I think it was a real reflection of the children born of the Thatcher era and taken obviously into a thriller genre. And after the success of that film Michael's position on film completely somersaulted and he virtually doubled my budget and let me get on with it and didn't interfere. And he was very pleased, clearly, to see that even if they couldn't show these films immediately nonetheless the publicity they generated for the channel and the high profile the films were now getting in cinemas was having a very good effect on the brand of Channel 4.

JS: *Tell me about your relationship with Andrew Macdonald,*[17] *John Hodge and Danny Boyle and the way that emerged, because looking back it's sort of easy to see how successive heads of Film Four had their own protégés that they've nurtured.*

DA: Andrew and John were involved initially and brought Danny in.

JS: *They auditioned for a director!*

DA: They did audition. I suggested they go and see three or four different directors, but clearly they found a soul mate at that period of their lives and it's sort of important that you find the right collaborators. And they clearly worked very well, at least for the first few years.

JS: *I read a story about one of them bribing your taxi driver to pass you the script of* Shallow Grave *on the way back to the airport!*

DA: They claim that they'd given it to my chauffeur. Well, it was news to me that I had a chauffeur! And it turned out they'd given it to my colleague Colin Leventhal, and so he gave it to me. I think I read it overnight and rang them first thing the following morning I was so excited. That's the thing about a screenplay, if you do respond to it you respond immediately and if you don't you may try to read beyond ten pages but it won't make any difference. You know, it's very hard to change the first initial response you have to the first ten pages. But I found it completely compelling and they were up in Edinburgh and I brought them down to London to talk it through.

JS: *I think you said that when Liz Forgan appointed you, she said that the only rule is you don't commission anything you're not passionate about.*

DA: It was my only sin. My only sin would be to commission something I wasn't passionate about.

JS: *So that sort of gut instinct about scripts is something that you still feel?*

DA: Yes, I think that's right, you've got to have that response because it's a long journey and if you don't have that initial response that stays with you through the journey, you keep wondering why am I doing this? Because most films, let's face it, do end in failure or relative failure, and so you've really got to believe in what you're doing, and some of them will work and many won't.

JS: *By the mid-1990s how many films a year were you making? A dozen?*

DA: I think it was more like fifteen, of which some would be relatively modest licences and some might be fully financed and some were in between the two for the balance.

JS: *Sort of a mixed slate, yeah.*

DA: And I absolutely believed in the importance of having a slate of at least that number of films in order to balance the film-makers between the beginners and the more experienced ones, the different genres and things like that, and also in terms of the outcome of the slate not to be dependent just on a few but to know that out of the fifteen if two or three really worked the slate would be successful as it were.

JS: *And, as you said, Michael Grade increased your budget during this time?*

DA: Yes. When I first arrived my budget was cut, there was an economic downturn, an advertising downturn, so my budget was cut. It was still, by today's standards, substantial. I think it was cut to something like six or seven million pounds a year for films which, ten or fifteen years ago, would have been more than Tessa [Ross] had to work with until relatively recently.

JS: *And indeed by the time you left the budgets were enormous, weren't they?*

DA: My budget for Film Four was £30 million I think by the time I left. Yes, and what it meant was not that we did massively more films, but it did mean that we were able to put more money into the same number of films and more money being put into films meant that editorially we would have more say as compared to other financiers.

JS: *That was characteristic particularly of the relationship you developed with Richard Curtis, wasn't it, because as I understand it the first film,* Four Weddings and a Funeral *(1993), Film Four had a relatively minor stake in because of Polygram's involvement with Working Title?*

DA: No, our total investment including the licence fee was £800,000 on a budget of £$2^1/_4$ to £$2^1/_2$ million.

JS: *Roughly a third.*

DA: Yes. And, interestingly, the part of the investment that wasn't the licence fee was collateralised against the territory where they thought the film would do least well, which was the United States of America. So in fact Film Four got paid out first because of that particular fluke. But in fact in later films of Richard's – I think with *Notting Hill* (1999) – we took a much smaller pot because there was no way they needed our investment. But they really did need it for *Four Weddings*, since Polygram weren't prepared to fully finance the film.

JS: *One of the people who was tremendously important to the team and had been there from the start was Colin [Leventhal], and although Colin's role changed he was very much a lynchpin of what the Film Four operation became.*

DA: Totally, you know, he was very much my partner in dealing with the business side largely, although I always respected his opinion with regard to films. But you know he did it brilliantly. And that was the wonderful thing about the job: you always felt that Colin and his colleagues were there to make things happen, not to stop things happening. And that was true of the lawyers, the business people, across the board, and that was a very positive environment in which to be working.

JS: *And working close to Wardour Street too?*

DA: There's something wonderful about that. When we moved into Horseferry Road,[18] the beautiful Richard Rogers building, we lost something of that informality, we were now suddenly an institution, whereas in Charlotte Street when a producer wandered in, our offices weren't that different from the conditions under which he or she was working, and there was an equality about that and that was lost but, you know, inevitably.

JS: *That's interesting because you allude there to the very particular role that Film Four has in terms of the ecology of the film landscape in this country. That commitment to discovering and nurturing talent, and of following a production through from script development right through to sales. How far did that inform what were you prepared to invest in development?*

DA: Well I had the full support of Michael Grade and the chairman that whatever problems we faced, and whatever cuts we faced, the development budget was never cut. That was part of our public remit, our public service remit, and we all took it very seriously.

JS: *And meanwhile, on the personnel front, you had, Jack left and Allon Reich came in. And of course you had Sara Geater as well on the team?*

DA: Sara was our Rottweiler!! She could detect people who were in trouble even before they knew they were in trouble and she kept a beady eye on budgets and production budgets and how funds were being spent and what was happening and she was invaluable.

JS: *I'm very interested in the kind of complimentary qualities of different personalities in a creative team. It's terribly important, isn't it, in film and television, that in a sense you have different characters who play different roles?*

DA: Yes, absolutely, and we were very different personalities but we did gel together. One of the things we all had in common was that we all wanted to make things happen, no one was trying to stop things happening, well you'd be surprised, often that is what you meet. And if people were in trouble Sara was always coming up with solutions and that was invaluable, because in many ways she was probably more experienced than most of the people that were working on these films, and so she could really help and get them through their problems. So you know, yes, it was a really terrific team we had there.

JS: *And indeed, the team was so good that you decided to branch out on your own? That was the HAL experiment, which was you and Colin and Allon, and Trea [Hoving], Colin's partner.*[19] *So what was behind that, was it a sense of, well, we've done what we can at Film Four now and we're kind of big and bold enough to strike out or was it the irresistibility of Harvey Weinstein and Miramax?*

DA: Well, we were courted by a couple of studios and so we thought that was probably the direction we should go in. I think clearly it didn't work out going with Harvey and ... it was a disaster!

JS: *Well, hindsight's a wonderful thing, but clearly at the time there was a sense in your thinking not only is this good for us but it's actually good for the British film industry?*

DA: We thought so. I mean certainly that's how Harvey sold it to us, and clearly he had a very good track record in supporting British films and supported a number of our Film Four films, so we hoped for a continuation of that.

JS: *And I think this unique relationship that film has with television in this country and the quite delicate balance that exists in its ecology provides a model of cultural subsidy that enables films to get made that otherwise wouldn't. I remember you saying to me that there's no reason to make a British film.*

DA: There's no market reason; the market isn't demanding a British film.

JS: *No, and cinema would survive in this country without.*

DA: It's true, and that is always a problem, so we have to fight for our existence, every day of every year, we can't build on our successes in the same way. You know, the French have a language, the Germans have a language, it separates them from Hollywood but we sadly don't and alas cinemas don't need British films to fill their screens. I mean they're delighted to have them when they're great, successful and popular but they're not, not in a way that in America the studios deliver films for a certain date in the calendar because that's when the cinemas want to be showing the latest blockbuster. We don't have anything like that in Britain.

JS: *No, it's an interesting and a very productive trade-off in a sense, isn't it? I mean, what you were saying earlier on about the fact that the broadcasters, Channel 4, the BBC, have recognised – it has taken the BBC a long time to recognise I think – that feature film is a tremendous showcase for your brand, particularly internationally, and the kind of trade-off with the broadcaster is OK we'll put some money into this and it's, you know, we can be seen to be doing something for the film industry, that sense of it being culture.*

DA: The synergy goes even further today than in my time when there was still a lingering prejudice against people who worked in television working in cinema and vice versa. Today I think it's accepted throughout the world really, you might do one project on television and another in cinema. You go between the two because of the project not because of the medium and there isn't a snobbism that used to exist. Now Scorsese, everyone, is very happy to work in TV as well as in film. So synergy is very important, you know it's great for a company like Channel 4 or the BBC to be working both in TV drama and film because there's a cross-fertilisation between the two media.

Paul Webster

Paul Webster was Head of FilmFour, 1998–2002.

Interviewers: Justin Smith and Laura Mayne
Interview: 23 April 2012

JS: *What was the landscape of the British film industry like when FilmFour was relaunched under Michael Jackson[20] and yourself? You uniquely worked with*

Palace and with Working Title for a bit, so in a sense you were the first person to occupy that Head of Film role that actually came from the film industry.

PW: In a sense, yes. But what you have to realise is that David Rose (from TV) was a founding father of the British independent film industry and Channel Four were a foundation stone. David Aukin (from theatre) carried on the good work and his success created the conditions that allowed me to have the freedom and responsibility I was given.

JS: *What was the kind of world Channel 4 created and what was their relationship like to companies such as Palace and Working Title?*

PW: By creating Film On Four, Channel Four effectively transformed their commitment to drama into film. The very first feature film I worked on, *Letter to Brezhnev* (1985), was a good example of the alchemy the channel wrought on a moribund industry. A tiny independent film from Liverpool, Channel 4's money made it possible for the film to get finished and also connected the inexperienced film-makers with the real world of distribution. Palace Pictures became involved with the film and the synergy between the three parties created a bona fide popular hit. During the 1980s almost all British independent films were supported by Channel Four Films. At Palace, which was a distribution *business*, we benefited immensely from our close ties with David Rose and Carol Meyer (who ran FilmFour International).[21]

When I started at FilmFour the brief was very much how to make it into a business, the interesting journey was, as they realised, they had some economic power. It had the trappings of a business under David Aukin but nevertheless he didn't have to answer to any economic brief whatsoever, so there was a slight contradiction there. At the time David was working under Michael Jackson for a little while and I remember Jonathan Olsberg[22] was commissioned to do a breakdown and an analysis of Film Four's strengths and weaknesses. David basically refused to answer any question he was asked about the economic value of anything he did, because he argued that he had no business case to answer because his brief was solely a creative one.

JS: *A wonderful vacuum to exist in!*

PW: Yes, and he exploited it and occupied it very well. So in those first sixteen years I was involved with Channel 4 Films quite a lot, firstly with Palace and then with Miramax. Miramax had a deep relationship with David Aukin, which included films like *Trainspotting* (1995) and *Brassed Off* (1996). Once I'd joined FilmFour, I kind of reciprocated and carried on the relationship with Miramax.

JS: *Was that Michael Jackson's vision? Did he come in with that brief and say, Paul, I want you to do this job?*

PW: The vision arose out of conversations we had together. The feeling was that Channel Four Films had had all this success and that it should be possible to have fiscal as well as creative rewards. Film Four under David had the trappings of business – international sales and UK distribution, but it was struggling to make money. The brief we gave ourselves was deceptively simple: 'make good films, make money'. I made some personnel changes in Sales and Distribution and created an acquisitions policy for third-party films for the UK distribution company then the next big challenge was to try and physically unite the staff – the company I took over had offices scattered all over Horseferry Road which was far from ideal.

JS: *It's like the psycho-geography of television is different from film.*

PW: That's right. Channel 4 were happy for us to relocate into a building in Fitzrovia, 60 people under one roof; Production, Sales, Distribution and Business Affairs all together. It was a terrific set-up that literally and figuratively distanced FilmFour from the rest of Channel 4. We supposedly had an arm's length business relationship with the channel but therein were sown the seeds of the idea's eventual demise: the programming demands of a broadcaster are often at odds with the needs of a film production and distribution company. We had a more commercial brief than our predecessors but because of our limited funding we frequently lost control of projects of a larger more commercial scale; in order to finance these films fully we needed partners who (as in the case of *Birthday Girl* (2001)) became majority financiers. We ended up the minority player and therefore with the minority voice on our own projects. If we had stayed within the comfort zone of the parent company we could have continued to produce films whose destiny we could control. We may have been better off. The problem for us, though, was that no one, least of all Michael Jackson, was interested in making a lot of little British movies that nobody went to see and nobody watched on television. The aim was to make larger, more international films. Our brief was to make critically acclaimed films that made money – easy!

Early on in my tenure we had a hit with *East Is East* (1999) which really was the perfect Channel 4/FilmFour film – distinct, populist, a critical smash and profitable. It was the British indie film of that particular time that broke out. The problem for us from a business point of view was that predicting *which* film was going to be the one to click was akin to searching for a needle in a haystack. There is no discernible pattern, it's luck, judgement and timing combined. In 1997 while working at Miramax I passed on *The Full Monty* (1997) at script stage. Somebody at Fox Searchlight didn't and they made the movie and a fortune.

JS: *Channel 4 passed on it as well.*

PW: They did. It wasn't possible to have a film company that made films in the comfort zone of Channel 4 that could in turn be commercially successful. We were in a difficult position and always had a compromised brief, for which I take quite a lot of responsibility. Also, Independent Film and Video was an experimental strand of film programming at Channel 4. Michael wanted me to take it over. I agreed on condition that the costs didn't appear in our P&L, that this was a purely creative venture. So we started Film4 Lab, we brought in Robin Gutch,[23] one of my heroes in the film business, and started making a lot of little movies, which sucked up a lot of our time and energy. Naturally, the numbers did hit our bottom line as the channel did not honour our initial agreement. Our relationship with Channel 4 became a bit of a poisoned chalice, which was complicated further by our ambitions being greater than our resources. One of the first things Michael and I did when I joined the company was to sit down with Michael Kuhn,[24] who at that time was just coming out of Polygram. In his opinion, the 34 million pounds worth of investment was only a fraction of what would have been required to make an impact in the marketplace. Of course, we didn't have anything like the resources nor was there any kind of appetite from our owners to raise that kind of capital. So you had this profit-driven company which couldn't really ever make a profit, it was destined to fail in that regard. But what it did do of course, when it was finally dismantled in 2002, was prepare the way for Tessa Ross to come in and take over, once again restoring the non-profit, non-economic brief which I believe is absolutely key to FilmFour's continuing success.

The money that comes from British film sources: Film4, BBC Films and now the BFI, is essential to the lifeblood of British independent cinema. Film is too expensive for an artist to produce in his garret and therefore you have to have some kind of industrial aspect to it and it costs. So then the only way it can work is to have benevolent organisations like Film4 to say, OK, we don't care about the money, we'll do it for the art anyway – which is what Tessa does. Tessa does care about the money sure, but ultimately she's the artist and the value of that may not be that great to people in the corridors of power at Channel 4, but I think in the film industry at large it's resonated forever. I think the results are there for all to see, I would argue right now we have more world-class directors in the UK than we've ever had, a great diversity of talent, fabulous actors, we've always had great actors but we continue to do so, we continue to grow them and it continues to consolidate Britain's place in the film world. It's of huge economic value, maybe not to Channel 4 or to the BBC, but to the industry in the country at large.

LM: *So you essentially had this pressure to provide films that would be commercially successful to Channel 4, but you also had this cultural commitment as well, while trying to provide space for new voices. Based on Channel 4's traditional film remit to provide a seedbed for new talent, how important was that to you at FilmFour? Was that a really firm part of your cultural remit?*

PW: Absolutely, we took the cultural remit very seriously. I mean we had to streamline it a bit because it was unmanageable. For example, there was originally a pledge to read every single script that came in, which I stopped. I have yet to read a single unsolicited script that's not come from a bona fide source that's of any interest at all, and if I miss the one that breaks through then . . . you have to be pragmatic. It was very interesting because we did to some degree change the remit in as much as there was a guarantee under David Aukin and David Rose before him, Mike Leigh, Ken Loach, Peter Greenaway, etc. got their money. Mike Leigh at the time was getting finance from Canal Plus in France. We tried to woo him back but failed. Ken Loach we did continue to support, with *My Name Is Joe* (1998), *Bread and Roses* (2000) and *The Navigators* (2001). *Bread and Roses* I wouldn't have supported but there was political pressure put on me to do so.

JS: *Where did the political pressure come from?*

PW: The Board of Channel 4, internal political pressure.

JS: *So although you were this autonomous organisation with a brief to make a profit, you were answerable to that kind of editorial pressure?*

PW: Yes, to some degree, I mean it was never consistent and generally we were left entirely on our own. Michael Jackson was a brilliant person to work for, the reason I took the job. Quite simply he's a film buff and wanted to have a film company. So it was kind of a little boy with his box of toys that gave us the opportunity. But just to go back to your question, we did mitigate our culture to some degree, I mean Peter Greenaway I didn't support at all and took the blast from him for that.

LM: *You used to support Terence Davies?*

PW: Yes, absolutely, and I'm very happy I did, a personal favourite of mine as a director.

JS: *His work also became more mainstream . . .*

PW: *The House of Mirth* (2000) was his first mainstream movie if you like, and that was an easy decision to make because under our funding structure for every movie we green-lit, Channel 4 gave us a million pounds for the cost of transmitting it on Channel 4. I was able to simply say to Terence, we'll put a million pounds into your film (knowing it was paid for by Channel 4) and if you can raise the other £5 million, then use this money as cornerstone finance. The movie worked very well for us, it sold well, it featured a fabulous performance from Gillian Anderson and it was a really fine film so it ticked all the boxes. I'm sure when it came to being broadcast by Channel 4 they put it on at 11 p.m. on a Sunday, which was the fate of many of our films. *My Name Is Joe* premiered at 1 a.m. on a Tuesday. Not only were we competing with the film buyers of Channel 4 whose job remit was to buy films, transmit them and buy TV rights, we were also competing with the Director of Programming in a way. I campaigned to re-establish Film on Four as a monthly 10 p.m. slot on a Sunday, which would showcase a FilmFour film. I failed miserably: it took me two years to get a meeting with the Director of Programmes, which lasted about 20 minutes and was disastrous. It wasn't a great atmosphere internally. Now senior level people like Dave Scott, Michael Jackson, Andrew Brann[25] and so on, no problem at all: full support. But on a day-to-day programming level, there was a disjuncture between film production and TV production.

In Europe, there is a different attitude regarding the broadcaster's relationship with film. I believe in Italy that RAI, the government station, is mandated to buy TV rights at pre-agreed prices. In France, Canal Plus have to give a proportion of their turnover to film production. Canal Plus is a cable TV subscriber-based company, and highly successful as a result. The model in the UK is kind of hybrid. The BBC and Channel 4 are mandated to support film production, but the value of the films they support has plummeted in the multi-channel digital age. The other thing to realise in terms of the cultural remit was that the major international relationship was with US companies like Miramax. The Americans of course had no such thing as a cultural remit, for them it was a matter of simply making business together. FilmFour's money was viewed as 'soft', money that simply reduces the budgets of film. It was a very complicated world within which to operate; it's always difficult for the person or organisation dispensing funds, which are viewed as public money. In fact Channel 4's money is not public money, the whole of Channel 4's income comes from advertising and the sales of the programmes internationally. I would say that a thousand times and nobody ever understood or listened, it's inexorably built into the national consciousness that Channel 4 is another version of the BBC.

LM: *Did anyone graduate from FilmFour Lab to write and direct FilmFours? Did it operate as a sort of seedbed in a way?*

PW: It would have, but it didn't have enough time to develop. If you're going to do that properly you need about a five-year programme and it was only around for three years. James Watkins came through that, Jamie Thraves sort of, a very talented film-maker. But when it came to guys like Jonathan Glazer or Edgar Wright, they went straight to big FilmFour, even though they were first-time film-makers.

JS: *But long term it wasn't sustainable?*

PW: No.

JS: *Because that seems to be one of the criticisms of FilmFour as a whole. The timescales required when setting up a project like that need to be much longer, and the terms of investment and underwriting need to have a much longer future; it was unrealistic to turn a profit in tomorrow.*

PW: Yes, it wasn't possible to do that. And particularly when we were continually a minority funder of films we had developed, which meant of course a minority share of whatever profits there were. But, you know, we were doing OK. There were two movies which ironically were touted as the reason the company fell apart: *Charlotte Gray* (2001) and *Lucky Break* (2001). Both made Film4 a lot of money using the pre-sales model, which is basically how independent movies are made in the UK, both were incredibly successful. The fact that they didn't work at the box office is another thing. One is always dealing with this disjuncture between the media perception and the business. The thing that you have to be very good at in the film business is burying your bodies, so we weren't very good at that ... too transparent.

JS: *Ironically* The Motorcycle Diaries *(2004) and* Touching the Void *(2003) which were snatched as it were from the jaws of defeat were hugely successful and great films.*

PW: Yes, it always seems to happen. It's a truism in film, the outgoing regime seeds the success of the next regime. We had *The Motorcycle Diaries*, *Touching the Void*, *The Last King of Scotland* (2006), *Shaun of the Dead* (2004), the list goes on. In fact, after a ten-year struggle, *Under the Skin* (2013) has just now been made which is one of the last of our films developed at the time. Luckily our legacy was a good one in terms of the projects we started. It provided the incoming management with a substantial base to work from.

JS: *What was the relationship between yourselves and Four Ventures, and were you in any sense answerable to Ventures or were you only answerable to Michael Jackson?*

PW: We only answered to Michael. Then when Michael moved out and headed to America, we became answerable to Four Ventures. But at that point the writing was on the wall, and Mark Thompson[26] had come on board and it was clear he wasn't too interested in the film side of things.

JS: *You think that was a kind of personal judgement? He wasn't as passionate about film as Michael was?*

PW: Yes, I think he made a very pragmatic decision and knew he needed to focus his energies in certain places and film was not a place he wanted to focus. You could look at the balance sheet in one way or another and you could say, well, OK, they're losing money we'll shut it down.

JS: *But Ventures as a whole was losing a lot more money.*

PW: Yes of course.

JS: *And to some extent film was scapegoated for that, wasn't it?*

PW: We were excoriated in the press. I don't care about it now but at the time it was a cause of much embitterment. There was a campaign in the press orchestrated by people within Channel 4 to besmirch FilmFour's name so that it became easier to shut it down. It was a very Machiavellian moment in time. I never held anything against Mark, he's a very straightforward man so he's actually very easy to deal with in a different way to Michael. But what was puzzling was the decision to shut the thing down at all. It didn't make any sense from an economic point of view because it cost a huge amount to close FilmFour down and then a month later start it up again.

LM: *In a Guardian interview in 2008 you said the closure of FilmFour was to do with a lot of factors but one of those factors was the failure of the main channel to essentially understand film financing. Could you perhaps discuss a bit more about that relationship?*

PW: Channel 4 at the time (it's important to realise this is just on the cusp of the digital revolution) was acknowledging the need to embrace this new multi-channel, multi-platform world, which in 1998 was only just beginning. The channel had won its argument with the ITV franchises and got full benefit of advertising income. It was a hugely successful company that was regularly turning in £350 to £500 million profit a year, all of which was ploughed straight back into the channel; they didn't take any profit at all, they simply reinvested. A perfect model. Once the multi-channel world came on stream, the advertising base eroded and thus the whole fiscal *raison d'être* of the channel. The only coherent response to every funding crisis was simply to go to government and ask for money. So there was Channel 4, not run as a business at all, but really a very good advertising sales outfit. There was no business model at all. I had a business model, which for the reasons I've laid out was in contradiction to what the channel wanted. It was kind of an impossible situation.

LM: *They always promised to invest more in film production if the ITV funding agreement came to an end, which they definitely lived up to.*

PW: Absolutely. We're not talking about a place where blood ran down the corridors, we're talking about a very benevolent organisation. Despite my moans and groans about the programming side of things, it was not a nest of vipers, it really was not. It was pretty gentlemanly and run in a mild-mannered way. I had come from the cutting edge of the film business and it was a kind of shock to me initially how things were run, how shambolic the infrastructure of FilmFour was. It couldn't possibly work if one was going to make a profit. So I set about kind of re-tooling that with the support of all the principals at Channel 4. It was in general applauded, but I think the only thing that matters is success and if I'd made loads of films which made loads of money and won lots of awards, then who knows, I could be there now. If Tessa had made a load of films which everyone thought well of but didn't make any money or didn't win any awards, she wouldn't be where she is now.

Tessa Ross

Tessa Ross was appointed Head of Drama at Channel 4 in 2000 and was Controller of Film and Drama, 2002–14.

Interviewers: Justin Smith and Laura Mayne
Interview: 1 August 2013

JS: *I understand when you joined Channel 4 from the BBC that you didn't come straight to film.*

TR: No, I came in as Head of Drama.

JS: *And FilmFour had been through this period of quasi-independence under Paul Webster. When you went for the Film4 job, was that a sense of this has come off the rails slightly, we need to get back to basics a bit, was that part of the kind of job description?*

TR: No, it wasn't really like that. The first thing was that the pressure on FilmFour Ltd was so huge because it was all about delivering cash, and secondly it was impossible for them to do that in such a short space of time. If you asked, 'were there some good films at that time?' you'd say, 'yes'. They made *Sexy Beast* (2000), *The Warrior* (2001), *The Motorcycle Diaries* (2004) to name a few – all great films. But their starting point was, 'We're going to have some hits.' And that was bloody difficult.

JS: *In the short term.*

TR: In the short term. And look, if they'd had enough money to pay for it for ten years it may well all have become brilliant. Why would it not be? But it was about the structure and the expectations placed on that organisation, and the fact that it wasn't just investing in production, it was also then doubling that money by spending it on distribution. Traditional British high-end films would not have been where Paul Webster's head was at that time because they would not have been hits – they would have been critical successes, but not hits.

JS: *So what was your idea?*

TR: The idea was to focus on the films. There was £10 million on the table. Everybody was gone. It was absolutely devastating – everybody wrote about FilmFour then that it was dead, it was defunct: 'the now-dead FilmFour' was what, if you Googled FilmFour, you got everywhere. And Channel 4 was eking out as slowly as possible the stock of films that it didn't want to play. So there were a number of issues. One was, Channel 4 needed to want the films that were made by FilmFour. It needed to want to play them, and it needed to feel its relationship with those films, rather than feel it was separate. In a way *Ali G Indahouse* (2002) had been the biggest example of that problem. That *Ali G* had gone to Working Title, having been developed as a character by Channel 4, seemed terrible. So the question was, how do you prevent those things happening? Of course you can't stop all of them happening, but you can be built in such a way that you encourage that synergy rather than lose it. So it was about having Channel 4 want the films, and having the talent that comes into Channel 4 believing that film is a possibility for them as part of their livelihood, and as part of their ambition. And having Film4 addressing its relationship to the industry. So we needed to look inside: 'How do we make you *want* from us?' And we needed to look outside: 'How do we make you want to be working with us?' So the fixing was sort of being an answer to these problems. What did the channel need? They needed good stuff that gets their name out in the world, and makes them look like they mean who they are. And what do the talent want? They need a collaborative, supportive, public service, British home that understands its own audience and its role among whatever other public money is out there. I mean that sounds very thought-through, and I probably didn't articulate it at all well at the beginning. But I basically said to Mark [Thompson], 'You have to write off £10 million, and I'll get you some good stuff on telly. Write it off, and I'll make sure that whatever we deliver at the very worst will look like Channel 4's heart on the telly. It may not be a hit in the cinema; it may not win you a prize. The worst version of it will be that when it comes back to the telly it will look like Channel 4. And I will be talking to talent that you want in the building, that is already in the building, and we'll be discovering new talent as well.'

LM: *This is a how long is a piece of string question, but how long would you say you spend at script development level at Film4?*

TR: Within the team a huge amount of time, a huge amount of resource. In our Development Team we've got three editors and a Head of Development, and an assistant who logs and coordinates everything. We've got some external readers and an intern who occasionally works with us, so it is a big resource to us. Because we understand that we're not cash rich, but what we can do is develop good material with producers, with or without directors, and build up enough of the kinds of material that Channel 4 needs to have, that Film4 needs to have, and also have ownership of that material. That's the only way that we could develop a project. We wouldn't start off thinking, 'Well we could make a $15 million movie.' Instead, we develop material with the producers and the talent, and then later down the line somebody else who believes in that material comes in and writes a cheque for it. It means that our small investment is delivering us huge value at the other end. If we didn't own the project up front we wouldn't get it, so what we've tried to do is spend time and money on development.

LM: *What proportion of your overall budget would you say you invested in development?*

TR: I would say it's just under 20 per cent.

LM: And is there a typical budget in your slate across films that are in development and films that are in production and being released, how do you balance that?

TR: Well, it balances itself, because I'm not in charge of when things are released. But if I said to you I've got 100 projects in development, we've probably got sixteen projects in various stages of production at any one time. And we've usually got eight or nine films just released or about to be released. It's a constant challenge really, and of the projects we're invested in at least 70 per cent are projects we've developed.

At least if not more. Which means if we didn't build them a lot of the films wouldn't get made. If we just sat around and said 'we'll take one of those', we wouldn't get what we wanted or we wouldn't get the films. So in a way we're definitely feeding a certain sort of flavour into the industry, there's no question. And that may be a good or bad thing, because who knows whether or not someone else would do it differently, or the flavour would be different. But given that our taste is to be adventurous and drive new talent, and be curious and at least edgier in some way, do things that other people wouldn't, there is a flavour that we are injecting into the industry which definitely has a different energy.

JS: *And to serve a public remit which has some of that at least enshrined in its core values, and has done from the start. Now you don't wait for scripts to come through the letterbox.*

TR: Yes, and we're extremely proactive. David Rose was the most wonderful Head of Film Four and is an example of how goodness and humanity can make talent grow. I mean it doesn't get better than that really, and he's such an exceptional human being. But at the time no one else was doing it in that way. Now we're competing as well as building, so we've got to do a bit of what David was doing – as well as we can, because none of us can be David – but equally we've got to grow, and we've got to deal with America a hell of a lot more, we've got to deal with other money a hell of a lot more; we've got massive commercial pressures on us. It requires a little bit of a different process.

JS: *And there's an independent film sector, which you're at the centre of, which there wasn't [then].*

TR: Exactly. And I think never rest on your laurels and think you're doing it the right way. There's isn't a meeting where we sit down and go, 'Aren't we clever, gosh that was easy.' We always sit down and go 'Gosh, what aren't we doing? And how do we make it alright? That sounds good and that sounds good, and we're not doing it, and why aren't we doing it, and how can we change that?' That doesn't mean to say we're always going to get it right, but that constant churn and expectation of change is really important.

JS: *And important to the vitality of a creative atmosphere. So how do you manage the workload across that team, in the sense, the Development Heads, do they have their own people?*

TR: Rose Garnett the Head of Development is new; she's completely brilliant. She seems to have an appetite for work like nobody I've ever seen – apart from Katherine Butler, who was until recently Deputy Head of Film, who also has the most amazing appetite for work. And you're surrounded by these people who have a massive passion, there's no jobsworth about it. And how does it work? Well, everybody feeds in ideas and we have a very rigorous development meeting, where everyone discusses who they're meeting, and what they've read, and who they've seen . . .

JS: *On a weekly basis or a monthly basis?*

TR: On a weekly basis. So Development is really in control of the development slate and we all throw into it. Their job is also to find those ideas and churn them – and we all feed in. If you imagine it's a lovely big basket where the Execs – Sam Lavender and Anna Higgs – and I, we all throw in ideas. And we follow that up with a development meeting where we talk about what we might want to green-light, whether it's worth green-lighting and how we might move it forward. We all get involved and talk about what we're doing. Then at the production stage I will make decisions along with my Exec team, but actually the development team will get involved here too.

JS: *So how soon would Sue Bruce-Smith get involved?*

TR: She's not really involved in early development – but she comes to editorial meetings, she reads scripts early on, we talk about ideas, we often talk about directors and producers, and matching people up. She's very involved the minute we decide to move things into production – in conversations about scale and value, and how things should be built, she's unbelievably involved.

JS: *I was going to ask you something about distribution actually, because this is something that interests me. You said it ages and ages and ages ago: that the problem is not getting British films made, it's getting British films seen. I know that during your tenure you've been involved in some quite imaginative ways of setting up some distribution arrangements and partnerships, as indeed have some of your predecessors with greater or lesser success. I mean how much power and influence have you got to move things on the distribution front, to influence the distribution sector, the distribution problem there seems to be in this country?*

TR: It's not easy, there's no silver bullet. The question you're asking is the right question – how do we make sure people want to see the films we make. We might be making the right films, but they're not the right films if nobody sees them. And as I said earlier the one good thing we've got is that we have the Film4 channel and we have Channel 4, and we can make sure that in some way those films are seen. But given that some of the films are small and new and without stars, how do we create the appetite? Which is why Film4.0 was built.[27] To ask ourselves, what can we do, what can we build around the films? I mean, of course it was about finding talent as well and making things differently, but part of it, the third leg of that set-up was, how can we make sure that we build around the films because distributors often aren't on board until very late? But the materials might be lost by then, the ideas might be lost by then, we might have to tell stories about some of our characters online and in order to create an appetite for the films, so that audiences do want to see them. So, it's so the right question. And I suppose the only thing I can say is that we're asking it all the time and trying to find different ways of answering it. Trying to address the windowing issue is a big part of what we're doing. We're working, I think, in really innovative ways with *Stone Roses: Made of Stone* (2013) or with ...

JS: A Field in England *(2013)?*

TR: *A Field in England* is a brilliant experiment, and doing it with a director who is such an adventurer, who is up for it, whose producers are up for it, who wants to understand how people consume his work because he's interested in audience, but he's also interested in film. Is it worth waiting for two years for a film that's been in cinemas? – no, it's not. The crass answer is always make films people want to see. But that isn't enough – because we haven't got the marketing budgets. So we've got to find ways of television driving VoD maybe – not always waiting for VoD and then television being at the end. It's just playing with that whole structure, and getting partners who are prepared to play with you. Because they're going to get it wrong as well as get it right. But I don't have an answer, I wish I had an answer!

JS: *No, no, in a sense you've provided lots of answers in the variety of different things you're doing. Clearly there isn't one thing – there is also the role of festivals, for example.*

TR: It's so interesting to me that the big films – the films that have success – have success almost all the time on the back of a successful

US release, which means that a UK filmgoing audience are influenced more than anything by American success, which is depressing. And how can we change that? Well, we understand British television – maybe there is something we should be doing differently that we're not yet doing. But we do need to keep asking that question.

JS: *Yeah, very much so. It's like we can only really believe something when it's sold back to us by the Americans.*

LM: *How important are European festivals like Cannes, how does reception and awards influence distribution here?*

TR: A lot of the films that go to those festivals have already got distribution. Obviously a lot of those films go there to sell. There are films we've made that have huge need of that launch, partly because they're sold to distributors at those launch festivals, partly because winning prizes allows people to feel confident about picking up or spending money on those films. So there is nothing that isn't useful for a small independent or medium-sized independent film.

LM: *I suppose it depends on the market, doesn't it?*

TR: And you just have to place it right and not kill your film before it's had a life. Because you can put your film in the wrong festival or in the wrong launch position, and it's gone before it's even existed. You know, that can happen too. So you do need people who think very carefully about the options.

JS: *This is a question that I've asked … well almost everyone we've spoken to … about this notion of what a typical Film4 is, and how, and particularly perhaps these days, how the Film4 brand is differentiated from BBC Films? They're no longer picking up Film4 rejects; they're the first port of call for some people.*

TR: What would you say about that?

JS: *I'm asking the questions!*

TR: No, but I'm really interested.

JS: *OK. I would say the word you used earlier, which was 'edgy', I think by and large they appeal to a slightly younger demographic than, say, BBC*

Films does. And I think often they're from the wrong side of the tracks or they fit with the multicultural – as it used to be called – diversity agenda in some ways. And I still think there's a remarkable continuity, it seems to me, across Film4's work, of, I don't want to say ticking those boxes because that sounds very functional, but of that kind of spirit. And attracting film-making talent of an age and a stage in its career when it wants to be edgy, it wants to find its voice.

TR: I think that's true for a lot of our output. I would say that the liberating thing about Film4 is that it is about film-making – it really is about film-making. Everything we make must sit on the channel – and it will sit on the channel if it's made with purpose as a film because that's what the channel believes in. And that means that Mike Leigh, who's still making films for us, is making films for us.

JS: *And he comes back to you.*

TR: I honestly believe that if there is a clear purpose and authorship, a sense of a need for resonance in the work that's being done, then it works for Film4. I would also say if you think you're a great film-maker and you've got something to say that no one else can say, then you should probably be working at Film4. We should be doing stuff that no one else can do, so there's a kind of comfort when people want to go to their truest place, to believe they're going somewhere that will defend the best essence of their work. That doesn't mean to say that the BBC doesn't make great work – it does. But it's very driven by the story and by its accessibility to the audience on television.

JS: *It's a kind of literary sensibility to film-making, I don't mean in a literary adaptation sense, but I think there's a kind of, there's literary qualities, character-driven narratives.*

TR: I mean I would ask you which of the films that the BBC made, that really you think should be or are Film4s? I can tell you what they are.

JS: We Need to Talk About Kevin *(2011).*

TR: Yeah. People congratulated me on that film all the time. *Fish Tank* (2009) too.

JS: Fish Tank, *yeah. And* Morvern Callar *(2001).*

TR: And why? Because they are about film-making. They're film-maker-driven films. And I find that really interesting. Brilliant that they were made, and I sort of think we probably would have made them, or should have made them, or could have made them. But it is quite clear that some films are right for the BBC and I've called up Christine [Langan][28] and said I think you should make this film. It's not because it's bad, it's not because I wouldn't love to go and see it.

JS: *And of course, they've got the great example of selling the BBC, the ability of films to sell the BBC brand in the States, which is fantastic and I mean which is one of the other benefits.*

TR: Film4 is a great brand because it's a recognised film brand, and BBC Films is still viewed essentially as a television brand. And I don't know enough about branding or about the BBC's rules about its own branding, but when you call something BBC Films you sound like you're talking about television. And when you say Film4 people know you're talking about film. And that's why we've had a hugely valuable boost, having a channel and having a brand, because Film4 channel can celebrate us, even if Channel 4 doesn't regularly put us in the same slot.

JS: *It's very clever actually, because at one time you had a very close relationship with the channel – a closer relationship than BBC Films has with television – and yet at the same time your brand identity is sufficiently robust that actually Film4 seems to be about making films.*

TR: But I do think it's been hard won.

JS: *It's evolved.*

TR: I don't think it was like that. It's been hard won, and I've now got a Chief Exec[29] who gets it, and that's made a massive difference. You cannot deny – ever – that you need the people around you to want it too. And in truth this is the first time somebody's said to me, 'I get how valuable what's going on here is.' You know, that your £15 million delivering £90–100 million-worth of film. That the brand, when it's visible, is brilliant on big films. You know fighting for branding on our big films has been hugely important. Having this talent talking about us without them asking to, is so wonderful. You know somebody getting up at a BAFTA ceremony and saying 'I'd like to thank Film4' is worth a fortune. We don't do advertising of ourselves. It's wonderful. It's about people feeling that they have a shared ownership because it's not about us, it's about them.

JS: *And a huge flagship for the channel of course.*

TR: *Exactly. And he gets it, and is very supportive. So it can take one person to come in and change that, for the BBC to get it right.*

LM: *Nowadays the government requires public service broadcasters to support the film industry, a situation that would have been unthinkable in 1982, when Channel 4 started. What does television's commitment bring to the British film industry?*

TR: I think it brings most of its films actually, doesn't it? It brings most of its public service support.

LM: *And can you see a scope for the expansion of television's involvement in film in the future?*

TR: Yes, I can. There's always an argument for where more money can exist, and where more visibility for films can exist. And given that we're talking about windowing, and how many more films will have that theatrical life. How many more films might reach their audiences sooner or differently on VoD and television? Of course those things will change. But I can't predict much further than that!

JS: *Yeah. But there's plenty of government support in the Policy Review that you yourself were involved with, wanting to get Sky on board and so on and so forth.*

TR: Yes. I think it's absolutely right that if you're making your money out of content, you owe it to this industry to build this industry. Not just this industry but public service television, not just film but television as well. And actually the truth is that it does seem odd to me to be able to come in and squeeze value out of the market without constantly putting it back in. And I think it's brilliant and right that Channel 4 is committed by licence now to make films. But then Channel 4's public service remit is onerous and big, and of course it makes it its special self. But it also has a huge commitment to an awful lot of duty, as does the BBC. So of course what you want is a vibrant, different range of possibility, from public service to completely commercial. But you do want there to be a duty to the next generation of talent, to the content industry of this country.

JS: *Absolutely. I think what's interesting, following on from that, is that over 30 years Channel 4 and latterly the BBC have forged a place, a sort of tier, a layer within the film culture that is unique. I mean it does exist elsewhere in Europe, but is unique as this kind of cultural subsidy, and I think that's hugely influential on the kinds of film that get made and the kind of film culture you have, and the kind of films that you've been talking about that wouldn't have existed otherwise, or would have perhaps existed differently otherwise.*

TR: And if you think that the people who we're working with in America, given that we're speaking the same language, and therefore can come and squeeze value, make money out of what we're doing – the pressure on them is for every dollar to deliver a bottom line. And that isn't the pressure on us. Of course that pressure grows and the market gets tougher in television, and commercial television particularly. But, in truth, if I made a tiny percentage back of what I invested but delivered great work, that would be OK, because that's my job. And that's the big difference between the pressure on Paul Webster and the pressure on us. Because I said, 'let me call it making great work rather than making money, and then we might get somewhere'. And that actually is a massive liberation, and of course that privilege does not exist anywhere else.

Notes

1. Sir Jeremy Isaacs was Chief Executive of Channel 4 (1981–7).
2. Channel 4 began broadcasting on 2 November 1982.
3. German-born actor and script consultant who became Channel 4's European representative and later Chief Executive of the European Script Fund.
4. German broadcaster Zweites Deutches Fernsehen.
5. David Rose was Head of English Regions Drama at BBC Pebble Mill, Birmingham (1971–81).
6. Colin Leventhal joined Channel 4 in 1981 as Head of Acquisitions. He became Head of Sales and Managing Director of Film Four International and was an Executive Director on Channel 4's board until 1998, when he left (with David Aukin, Sara Geater and Allon Reich) to form the UK Miramax subsidiary HAL.
7. Sara Geater was Co-production Executive in Drama and Film at Channel 4 between 1984 and 1998 and returned as Head of Commercial Affairs from 2004 to 2007.
8. Walter Donohue was a commissioning editor for Fiction at Channel 4 (1982–86).
9. Karin Bamborough was a commissioning editor for Fiction at Channel 4 (1982–90).
10. Michael Kustow was Commissioning Editor for Arts Programmes at Channel 4 (1982–9).
11. Peter Ansorge worked with David Rose at Pebble Mill and became Commissioning Editor for Drama Series at Channel 4 (1987–97). Michael Wearing joined BBC

Pebble Mill in 1976 as a script editor and became a producer. In 1989 he was made Head of Serials at the BBC. Tara Prem also worked as a script editor at Pebble Mill and later as a BBC drama producer.

12. Sarah Radclyffe was co-founder of Working Title Films (1983–92).
13. Liz Forgan was Channel 4's Senior Commissioning Editor for Current Affairs and later Director of Programmes (1981–90).
14. Michael Grade was Chief Executive of Channel 4 (1987–97).
15. Jack Lechner was script editor and commissioning executive at Channel 4 (1992–6).
16. Stephen Woolley was co-founder (with Nik Powell) of Palace Pictures (1982–92).
17. Producer Andrew Macdonald formed Figment Films in 1993 working with screenwriter John Hodge on a series of films directed by Danny Boyle, including *Shallow Grave* (1994), *Trainspotting* (1995), *A Life Less Ordinary* (1997) and *The Beach* (2000). He established DNA Films (1997) in partnership with Duncan Kenworthy.
18. Channel 4 left its original home at 60 Charlotte Street in 1994 to move to new, purpose-built premises at 124 Horseferry Road.
19. HAL was a short-lived UK subsidiary of Harvey Weinstein's Miramax, which did much to support British film during the 1990s.
20. Michael Jackson was Chief Executive of Channel 4 (1997–2002).
21. Carol Meyer was a film sales agent at Channel 4 (1982–6). She was succeeded by Bill Stephens.
22. Jonathan Olsberg is a film producer and chairman of media strategy consultants Olsberg SPI who were commissioned to produce a report on Channel 4's contribution to the UK film industry in 1997.
23. Robin Gutch was a commissioning editor in the Independent Film and Video Department at Channel 4 and ran the FilmFour Lab, an innovation hub for low-budget independent film (1993–2003).
24. Michael Kuhn joined Polygram NV in 1975 and in 1991 established Polygram Filmed Entertainment which went on to make and distribute more than a hundred films. In 1999 he set up the independent production company Qwerty Films.
25. Andrew Brann joined Channel 4 in 1986 as a Programme Acquisitions Executive, becoming Head of Co-productions and later Head of Business Affairs. He left the Channel in 2004.
26. Mark Thompson was Chief Executive of Channel 4 (2002–4).
27. Film4.0 was a low-budget digital film initiative established in 2011 under Commissioning Executive Anna Higgs. It pioneered the user-generated competition Scene Stealers, developed documentary projects with Carol Morley (*Dreams of a Life*, 2011) and Ken Loach (*The Spirit of '45*, 2013), worked with Warp Films and Shynola on the Vimeo short *Dr Easy* (2013), and produced Ben Wheatley's *A Field in England* (2013). From 2014 its digital innovation activities are being incorporated into Film4.
28. Christine Langan was appointed Executive Producer at BBC Films in 2006 and, since 2009, has been its Creative Director.
29. David Abraham was appointed Chief Executive of Channel 4 in 2010.

BOOK REVIEWS

Jonathan Murray, *Discomfort and Joy: The Cinema of Bill Forsyth* (Bern: Peter Lang, 2011), pp. 270, ISBN 3039113917 (pb), £35.

The career of Bill Forsyth is central to Scottish film, and yet this book, written over a decade after Forsyth's last film to date, can bill itself on its back cover as 'the first integrated and comprehensive study of the director's complete oeuvre'. There has been no lack of attention to Forsyth, but when that writing has been as part of a consideration of Scottish film it has tended to look at questions of Scottishness while passing over his work in America. As the bulk of the remaining writing on his work has been in reviews, there has been little in the way of a broad overview. *Discomfort and Joy* attempts to put one together, summarising the various critical opinions on each of Forsyth's films in turn, chapter by chapter. These take the form of redemptive readings, aiming to free each work from interpretations based on truisms, and showing how each fits within the whole of the director's *oeuvre*.

That career is almost ready-made for study, with his eight films to date breaking neatly into a Scottish first four, then three in America, with a Scottish sequel as a late coda. Redemptive readings, as it transpires, are very necessary, because certain critical misunderstandings or even dismissals of Forsyth's work have become common. Tracking the critical response to Forsyth chronologically allows Murray to identify how such misconceptions have arisen. The study is necessarily exhaustive – Murray seems to have read, and needed to read, every article on Forsyth – but it proves to be a rewarding one. The early chapters look in some detail at the financing – a necessity given how stunted these films' budgets were, but one which also enables Murray to show how this affected them critically. *That Sinking Feeling* (1979) and *Gregory's Girl* (1981) were both written to accommodate casts predominantly made up of young actors, allowing the films to be made cheaply. But this coloured their reception.

Journal of British Cinema and Television 11.4 (2014): 552–566
Edinburgh University Press
© *Journal of British Cinema and Television*
www.euppublishing.com/jbctv

By *Gregory's Girl* – only his second feature – Forsyth was being chided by some critics for failing to mature as an artist. Murray notes that a problematic vocabulary developed: 'The familiar adjectival roster used to describe this and other Forsyth movies – charming, whimsical, light, wry, pawky, eccentric, gentle, delicate, slight – carries with it a decided whiff of infantilisation' (44–5). This roster, assembled early, was to follow Forsyth's career to the point at which the later films, particularly *Comfort and Joy* (1984) and *Housekeeping* (1987), were seen as somehow 'lesser' because they couldn't be described simply by this stock lexicon.

Murray also establishes early that Forsyth is not merely a comic Scottish film-maker, but a film-maker who can use Scottishness or comedy, or whichever other elements he chooses to work into his films, as part of a personal take on the genre in which he happens to be working. This take does include a notable strain of melancholy, and although Murray initially seems to overstate this as 'an idea of the human condition as an existentially lonely one' (3), his analysis throughout the book gradually builds a convincing case for this assertion.

Indeed, the author typically makes his cases strongly throughout, with each essay taking on Forsyth's harshest critics, even when, for example, the critic who called *Breaking In* (1989) a 'bastard child' (167) is Forsyth himself. 'The present discussion', Murray notes coolly, 'does not dismiss *Breaking In* thus' (167). What follows is one of the more successful essays in establishing grounds for praising a film that has been neglected. A previous chapter, on *Comfort and Joy*, positions that film as a critique of Thatcherism, one which shows the effects of privatisation on individuals, unlike other British films of the time – for example, *Defence of the Realm* (1986) and *The Ploughman's Lunch* (1983) – which addressed the political process directly. With *Breaking In*, Murray first carefully establishes that while the film was based on John Sayles' script, Forsyth rewrote it to his own design. This enables an interpretation where the film can be seen as a quietly deliberate subversion of the buddy movie genre, with a bittersweet ending of a sort Forsyth has often employed. This commonality allows Murray to reclaim this particular film as part of Forsyth's *oeuvre*, though it is the one film on which he is not credited as a writer. The author similarly shows how Forsyth's adapted screenplay for *Housekeeping* differs from the original, particularly in ending earlier in the storyline than did the book, in a way which reveals Forsyth's hand at work.

Redemptive readings prove to be more awkward in considering *Local Hero* (1983) and *Being Human* (1994), although both essays are still valuable. *Local Hero*, as the most critically lauded of Forsyth's works, hardly needs to be redeemed. Murray does try arguing against critics who depicted it as 'Ealing-Scottish' (75) that the film actually subverts this description, but this is overturning an argument which is particularly weak in the first place. On the other side of the critical spectrum, *Being Human* is somewhat beyond redemption, disowned by both Forsyth and Warner Brothers after both parties negotiated a final cut that neither fully endorsed. Murray attempts to move past wrangling about the film's flaws to discuss what its message is, but it's a tentative step at best. Nonetheless, while the redemptive aspect of these essays stalls, the analysis of directorial themes and the detail that Murray provides about the making of both are typically excellent.

Murray's style of criticism treats each work as a text created by Forsyth, which can then be analysed as such. This is a useful critical approach, though it can seem odd, for example, to read an essay on *Local Hero* that never mentions Mark Knopfler's score. Nonetheless, this book fulfils its stated remit as both a summation of the critical consensus of Bill Forsyth's work, and as an advance on that consensus by examining that work as a whole. Though a fuller picture of the film-maker as a collaborative artist is possible, this book must be the starting point for any serious study of Forsyth that follows.

Keir Hind (freelance writer and editor)
DOI: 10.3366/jbctv.2014.0233

Sarah Street, *Colour Films in Britain: The Negotiation of Innovation 1900–1955* (London: BFI/Palgrave Macmillan, 2012), pp. iv + 316, ISBN 9781844573127 (pb), £19.99.

'One is starved of Technicolor up there', says Marius Goring of heaven, as he plucks a pink rose from an earthbound bush in *A Matter of Life and Death* (1946). It is one of the most famous lines from one of the most notable examples of British colour film-making, and one that Sarah Street quotes three times in her study of British colour film in the first half of the twentieth century. But down here, at least in cinemas, as demonstrated in this extensive book, the British were exploiting colour to its fullest potential. *Colour Films in Britain* charts 55 years of colour film production and exhibition, tracing technical developments as well as aesthetics, and incorporating this film technology within discourses about national character and artistic identity.

Starting with the emergence of the first technically and commercially viable colour system used in the UK, Urban and Smith's Kinemacolor, Street covers the development of the technical processes by which colour cinematography was achieved, as well as offering detailed readings of the use of colour in a number of key texts. The latter include both acknowledged classics (case studies of the colour films of The Archers inevitably, but justifiably, dominate the latter half of the book) and more obscure films that hold an important position in the development of the art and craft of the colour film. However, the focus is almost wholly on British film productions, with foreign films (including many Hollywood titles) discussed only in passing. Street considers how colour was used to add narrative value, but also how colour fitted with ideas of culture, values, patriotism, glamour and – with particular reference to The Archers and producer Alexander Korda – the exotic.

The larger part of the book covers films shot in Technicolor's three-strip System 4 process, a format that seems to hold an almost mystical fascination for certain film historians. Street herself exhibits some of these tendencies, citing vague theories that the chemicals – and even the water – used in this country had created a distinctive colour rendition in the negatives and prints emerging from Technicolor's UK labs (87). However, in other regards Street gives very precise and clear examples of the impact of different colour processes, such as the limited colour palette of Duyfacolour's single negative system fitting with *Sons of the Sea*'s (1939) restrained domestic drama, in comparison with the emphatic exoticism of such adventures as Alexander Korda's imperial epics such as *The Four Feathers* (1939) and *The Thief of Bagdad* (1940). In addition, she attempts to re-evaluate the reputation and contributions of Natalie Kalmus, the Technicolor consultant credited on almost all Technicolor productions. Kalmus still emerges as a controversial figure, whose involvement, or interference, was regarded by many directors and cinematographers as at best an irrelevance and at worst a positive hindrance to producing good work. But debates about her contribution at the time and since are dominated by the palpably sexist attitudes to a woman of considerable power and confidence in what remains a male-dominated industry.

Street's study stops in the 1950s. This is probably not an arbitrarily chosen end point; it is when three-strip Technicolor was rendered obsolete by the arrival of widescreen processes such as Cinemascope, with which the three-strip process was incompatible, and improved 'monopack' single negative colour film stocks such as Kodak's Eastmancolor. However, Street doesn't actually justify this cut off point, and therefore misses a valuable opportunity for discussion of the impact of Eastmancolor on production practices, or of the effect of the more realist-minded film-making of the early 1960s 'kitchen sink' directors. Such coverage would have been more useful than the occasional digressions into the realms of high film theory, given the otherwise rigorously historical perspective of the writing. For example, it would have been instructive to read an analysis of how Michael Powell had adapted to Eastmancolor and the lurid demands of the horror genre in *Peeping Tom* (1960) after the high-brow tone of *The Red Shoes* (1948) and *The Tales of Hoffman* (1951), and the visual glories of three-strip Technicolor.

Of course, this is asking for a longer version of what is already a sizable and exhaustively researched book. Of particular value is the way in which it discusses film colour not merely in the context of the canon of accepted classics and through the usual auteurist prism, but also in the context of the culture of the time, drawing in discussions of animation, industrial film, documentary, fashion, even interior design and horticulture, thus placing film within a culture of colour beyond the cinema auditorium. Street's wide-ranging sources include contemporary reviews and criticism, which provide valuable insights into how these productions were considered at the time, as well as snippets from Mass Observation surveys charting popular opinion. The excerpts from writers such as E. S. Tompkins, a columnist in the *British Journal of Photography* whom Street rightly describes as 'extraordinarily astute', display a strong grasp of the complexity of expression possible in a popular art form and, as Street writes, 'constitute a fascinating record of responses to colour film' (71).

However, Street does have some odd habits as a writer, such as an occasional tendency to use the word 'notorious' when she must surely mean 'notable', and 'infamous' when she means simply 'famous' – for example Powell and Pressburger's 'infamous "stairway to heaven"' (133). In general, though, the book is clearly and lucidly written, even if it does take for granted a familiarity with the films; the density of the researched material means there is little space for the plot synopses or biographical information on the key figures that a more casual reader might expect from such a mainstream publication. The book is pitched at the reader with a confident knowledge of the films and film culture of the time, and with a keen and patient interest in the arcane details of the technical processes by which the cinematographic image is created.

The book concludes with extensive appendices covering the huge range of colour formats developed across the period, as well as listing colour films (both British and foreign) released in the UK from 1938 to 1955, chiming again with the heyday of three-strip Technicolor. It is packed with well-chosen colour images and, importantly, they are actual frame enlargements from the films themselves, not production publicity stills. Street chooses the frames well, using them to illustrate specific creative and technical choices. However, the quality of the reproduction is not always high. Certain of the images look as though they have been taken from video sources (possibly DVDs), and many have a murky, washed-out patina that does not do justice to the qualities of the original imagery. That said, this is an understandable compromise which has kept the cover price down, as the use of glossy colour plates would have resulted in a far more expensive book.

Dylan Pank (University of Portsmouth)
DOI: 10.3366/jbctv.2014.0234

Andrew Moor, *Powell and Pressburger: A Cinema of Magic Spaces* (London: I. B. Tauris, 2012), pp. xii + 250, ISBN 9781780763774 (pb), £12.99.

The centenary of Michael Powell's birth in 2005 witnessed an increased interest in the work of the late film-maker. Along with a host of commemorative activities, such as film screenings at the National Film Theatre and a special edition of *Screen*, came the publication of four books assessing the work of Powell (three of which also focused on the input of his long-time partner, Emeric Pressburger). Andrew Moor's *Powell and Pressburger: A Cinema of Magic Spaces*, now available in paperback, was one of the four books published that year that sought to build on the work of Ian Christie in recognising the film-maker's important contribution to the British film industry. Thought-provoking, well-researched and lucidly written, Moor's book reminds us of what the book's cover rightly calls the 'remarkable and visionary' quality of Powell and Pressburger's body of work, and is essential reading for anyone interested in the films made by two of British cinema's most remarkable innovators.

A Cinema of Magic Spaces is organised into six thematic chapters covering Powell and Pressburger's early output, wartime propaganda films, pastoral dramas, 'male' films, 'female' films and their 'art' productions. Moor's aim is to explore the 'magic spaces' that populate Powell and Pressburger's work. As he explains, it is not the physical spaces that this book surveys, but imagined terrains, borders, conflicting loyalties, changing national and gender identities, and longing for vanished homelands. Such an approach could reduce the duo's films to a series of abstract structures, but Moor is careful to place them within the film-makers' cultural and historical environments, thereby rooting their output. For example, the social changes wrought by the Second World War are shown to have been carefully rendered in many of the duo's films; the 'mythical community spirit' (78) evident in Launder and Gilliat's *Millions Like Us* (1943) and Carol Reed's *The Way Ahead* (1945) is thus equally present, Moor contends, in Powell and Pressburger's *The Life and Death of Colonel Blimp* (1943). Moor also draws attention to the importance of J. Arthur Rank's 'hands-off' approach in contributing to The Archers' success, describing the film baron as 'a bountiful and yet detached patron' (21). As Moor contends, being given significant creative freedom permitted Powell and Pressburger the space in which to experiment with their style (as it did with other production companies in Rank's empire, such as Gainsborough, whose costume melodramas were the major British box-office successes of the mid to late 1940s), thus allowing them to become the master film-makers of their time.

This acknowledgement of the importance of creative freedom could have been pushed further, however, as could the broader production background which, for the most part, is left relatively uncharted. It would have been interesting, for example, to discover more about the behind-the-scenes activities of the studio, or how Powell and Pressburger managed to circumvent censorship restrictions at a time when both the Ministry of Information and the British Board of Film Censors commanded significant control over film content. Similarly, while Moor does draw attention to the films' historical contexts – in particular in Chapters 4 and 5 which begin with a description of the historical and cultural background – it would have been more successfully historicised if this context had fed more closely into the film analyses.

Despite this limited attention to the production background, the real strength of this book is Moor's lengthy and detailed appreciation of Powell and Pressburger's body of films. Keenly aware of the artistic merit of the duo's output, Moor's critical commentaries are both fascinating and informative. Drawing on the work of a broad range of cultural theorists (Pierre Bourdieu, Antonio Gramsci and Raymond Williams, to name but a few) to underpin these analyses, Moor reveals that while the films of Powell and Pressburger are 'notably experimental and thematically complex' (3), there is clear continuity between them: messages recur, symbols persist, ideals are cemented.

The two principal recurring themes that Moor identifies circulate around identity – specifically national and gender identities. Rather than viewing these identities as fixed, Moor reveals how the film-makers played on their constructed nature, recognising the diversity and fluidity of both forms of identity. In *The Life and Death of Colonel Blimp*, for example, Moor reveals how national identity is presented as 'a matter of imaginative investment', one formulated by a 'collage of historical elements' (61). By doing so, Moor contends, wartime audiences could relate the film's narrative to the contemporary situation, and the actions of its protagonist, Clive Candy, to their own. In *A Matter of Life and Death* (1946), meanwhile, Moor suggests that the dissolves in the court case sequence 'suggest the geographical fluidity of national identity' (148) that permitted audiences the chance to relate their postwar experiences to those of the assembled characters on the screen. The postwar 'art' films, *Black Narcissus* (1946) and *The Red Shoes* (1948), are similarly shown to have explored the amorphous state of identity – this time gender identity – thus closely aligning them to the period's emergent cultural dynamics in which both femininity and masculinity were tested and their 'certainties' questioned.

Informative and illuminating though these critical commentaries are, there is, however, an imbalance in their analyses of Powell and Pressburger's output. While certain films are afforded a good deal of coverage (*The Life and Death of Colonel Blimp* and *Black Narcissus* are each awarded a whole chapter), others are skimmed over rather rapidly (the discussions of *I Know Where I'm Going* (1945) and *The Tales of Hoffman* (1951) take up only a few pages), with the result that the structure of the book is a little uneven. It would have also benefited from the inclusion of a concluding chapter. While it comes to a 'natural' end by focusing on the later work of the film-makers, a specific conclusion would have helped to draw together all the many threads that Moor so fascinatingly lays out in the preceding chapters. Nonetheless, despite these structural weaknesses, Moor's astute reading of Powell and Pressburger's output (which also profitably includes an intriguing exploration of the duo's unfilmed material) provides an absorbing insight into the ways in which these film-makers worked, and consequently offers much useful information for students, academics and the general public alike. This paperback edition makes it an accessible book for all.

Robert James (University of Portsmouth)
DOI: 10.3366/jbctv.2014.0235

Stella Hockenhull, *Aesthetics and Neo-Romanticism in Film: Landscapes in Contemporary British Cinema* (London and New York: I. B. Tauris, 2014), pp. 288 + 14 illus., ISBN 9781848859012 (hb), £58.

Stella Hockenhull's book *Aesthetics and Neo-Romanticism in Film: Landscapes in Contemporary British Cinema* sets out to try to make us consider British films not only in terms of their narratives and themes but also of their pictorial qualities and, in doing so, to engage with the emotional effect of particular landscape shots on the spectator. Other writers such as Rachael Low and Andrew Higson have already noticed the different (but also ultimately linked) pictorial/narrative trajectories in British cinema history, but Hockenhull's key innovation is to try to encourage us to engage with the 'pictorial' through the type of aesthetic theory that developed in the field of philosophy and was applied specifically to the visual arts. As Hockenhull puts it: 'To offer an interdisciplinary approach between the visual arts facilitates an acknowledgement of wider cultural and social issues, and in addition some recognition of contemporary anxieties' (209). On the surface this appears to be a worthy and perhaps even important project. At its heart is Hockenhull's own ability to draw on art history, which is often fairly impressive in its application – as was demonstrated by her earlier monograph *Neo-Romantic Landscapes: An Aesthetic Approach to the Films of Powell and Pressburger* (2008). This new book is in some ways laudable in its ambition. Hockenhull sensibly draws on the excellent work of writers such as Martin Lefebvre on cinema and landscape in order to attempt to do something genuinely fresh and interdisciplinary with British cinema. But the book is not without significant problems.

The chapters are organised around distinct themes which are loosely linked to genres. So, Chapter 1 deals with realism, locating the 'pleasurable lure' (35) of landscapes in five loosely realist films, including *Sweet Sixteen* (2002) and *Better Things* (2008). Here Hockenhull uses Caspar David Friedrich's *Rückenfigur* – the isolated figure in a sublime landscape, usually with their back to the viewer – to offer some often illuminating readings of these films which allow us to think about them in new ways.

Chapter 2 deals with 'sublime' horror. This is perhaps the strongest chapter in the book. Here Hockenhull makes rich links between examples of modern British visual art and depictions of landscapes in a range of contemporary British horror films. Drawing on Edmund Burke's concept of the sublime, Hockenhull demonstrates how far films such as *The Last Great Wilderness* (2002) and *Eden Lake* (2008) seemingly develop representational strategies which have also been evident in the visual arts, in some cases for centuries. This chapter also picks out various intriguing tensions between the narratives of these horror films and their evidently pictorial qualities.

Chapter 3 focuses on female figures in landscapes. Here Hockenhull writes about the issue of prospects and perspectives that have tended to operate historically from a masculine point of view. She usefully reminds us that Burke himself gendered the sublime as masculine and beauty as feminine. These types of tensions clearly endure in contemporary British cinema, as she demonstrates.

Chapter 4 deals with 'accented cinema' (borrowing Hamid Naficy's term) – films directed by film-makers with non-British roots – and notices themes of escape, nostalgia and yearning for homelands being worked through in depictions of often peripheral contemporary British landscapes, such as the grim Stonehaven/Margate of Pawel Pawlikowski's *Last Resort* (2000).

So, there is some good work here. But the book does have significant problems. One of the key drawbacks is its lack of any useful outline of what precisely aesthetic theory is and how, historically, it has been employed. Hockenhull devotes no more than a paragraph to this – briefly discussing Edmund Burke – before moving on to explore Geoffrey Nowell-Smith's (admittedly pertinent) thoughts on the notion of the aesthetic study of film. It was very surprising not to see mention at least of Theodor Adorno's work here, for example on the concept of 'Natural Beauty'. This might have proved very useful in the readings of some of the films.

Moreover, there are a number of potential problems inherent in adopting an 'aesthetic' approach to reading films. To her credit Hockenhull does acknowledge this, but unfortunately the book can never quite shake off the presence of these problems, or at least engage with them to any useful degree. Hockenhull reminds us that André Bazin once compared cinema to painting in a 1950 essay (16). But films are not paintings. Films are images, edited together, often with different camera angles that develop different perspectives. Films are also of course mechanically reproduced texts that are exhibited in a range of ways, all of which are different from paintings and thus lacking their uniqueness and 'aura' (as Walter Benjamin famously noted). Cinema is also of course a collaborative cultural form, which might well be artistic but is largely industrial and commercial. In order to argue the case for employing aesthetic theory, Hockenhull attempts to work through ideas such as the *temps mort* in film (Martin Lefebvre). But we need to remember – and indeed the book ultimately reminds us – that there is no getting away from the fact that, at its heart, cinema is perceived as moving images, even if, strictly speaking, it is not comprised of moving images as such. This does not mean that we should not analyse the film frame, but it does mean that aesthetic theory – as it has been applied to visual art – certainly has its limitations and that these need to be critiqued very carefully indeed. This book does not ever do this properly.

At its worst the book too often appears to lose sight of a single coherent objective. A lack of clarity is perhaps evident in the rather clunky title: *Aesthetics and Neo-Romanticism in Film: Landscapes in Contemporary British Cinema* is too complicated to be properly focused and thus useful. It certainly suggests that the book may be trying to do too many things at once. A book simply titled *Landscapes in Contemporary British Cinema* might have sufficed here. If the book really was to be about film landscapes, then by placing 'aesthetics' at its heart Hockenhull perhaps narrowed her potential avenues in this area. If instead the key focus of the book is indeed aesthetics (and it does seems that this is the case), then why is Hockenhull concentrating on British films only? The same might be said for the term 'neo-romanticism', which is never properly adumbrated within the contexts of British cultural history. Is it really true to say that that all of the films she talks about do actually have neo-romantic elements? If so, what does this mean at the level of representations of contemporary Britain and Britishness? Furthermore, the 'Britishness' of the representations of landscape under discussion is never really adequately dealt with either. What is it that feels specifically British (or otherwise) about the landscapes under discussion? It is important to recognise that some of the aesthetic theory that Hockenhull introduces suggests a rich northern European tradition of representation – not just simply British (see Friedrich's *Rückenfigur*, as mentioned above). This fact ideally needed to be engaged with more carefully. In the drive to discuss aesthetic approaches to film, then, Hockenhull does not ever adequately explain why British films in particular warrant such an approach, nor indeed does she properly consider what the possible ramifications of such an approach might be.

In her Introduction, Hockenhull writes: 'For the purpose of this book, the ways in which the landscape is formally structured by the film-maker and technical staff, whether intentionally or not, elicit an emotional response from the spectator and relate to the notion of affect' (9). There are a number of problems inherent in this statement. Firstly, if we are to talk of the emotional 'affect' of films, how is this 'affect' to be theorised or indeed measured? While in the Introduction Hockenhull argues that we need to understand how moving images elicit emotion (whether or not as an intention of the film-maker), the notion of 'affect' is barely dealt with throughout the main chapters. Certainly, while mention is made in the Introduction of David Bordwell's work on the activity of the film viewer, and of Jennifer Harding and Deidre Pribram's work on emotion as power, the work of important theorists in this area (Deleuze and Guattari,

Carl Plantinga, Giuliana Bruno, Steven Shaviro, for example) is either not drawn upon adequately, covered or even mentioned. Certainly no attempt is made in useful terms here to deal with 'affect' at the level of spectatorship, and Hockenhull does not draw on extant scholarly work on film spectators or, indeed, audiences. Furthermore, throughout the book there is little or no engagement with the issue of intentionality. For example, where possible it might have been useful to interview the film-makers and, especially, the cinematographers (who are barely mentioned) about their vision, or at least their intentions regarding how these landscapes were to be framed in the films. And more might have been said about how sound and music impact upon the representation of landscape, too – although to Hockenhull's credit this much is admitted in the Conclusion.

But the Conclusion is not strong. A clear adumbration of the findings of the book was really necessary here. Instead Hockenhull offers more points covering a rapid succession of texts and loosely linked thoughts on contemporary art exhibitions, among other things, which do not properly serve to conclude, or at best sum up, the points raised throughout the four chapters. There is certainly no attempt here properly to reflect on affect and emotion (so tantalisingly mentioned in the Introduction). Having said this, Hockenhull does briefly reflect on the efficacies of the aesthetic approach to studying film, sensibly admitting that, despite the necessity to 'embrace as wide a perspective as possible' (209) when reading a film, this approach, when adopted alone, is ultimately not always particularly satisfactory.

Despite these criticisms, this remains a useful book that encourages us to look at British films with new eyes. What we have here is a series of sometimes insightful critical analyses of contemporary films by a scholar who is attempting to do something interesting and even perhaps important – to move towards a more nuanced engagement with the pictorial elements in British cinema, and to think more carefully about the full range of potential pleasures that even the seemingly grimmest films might offer us. At its best this book is an ambitious attempt to reinvigorate British film studies, and to shift it towards a more interdisciplinary appreciation of spatiality, and of film, emotion and affect. It also in some ways signals the potential for further interdisciplinary work which might bring British film studies, cultural geography, philosophy and art history closer together.

Paul Newland (Aberystwyth University)
DOI: 10.3366/jbctv.2014.0236

Paula Blair, Old *Borders, New Technologies: Reframing Film and Visual Culture in Contemporary Northern Ireland* (Bern: Peter Lang, 2014), pp. xx + 271, 30 illus., ISBN 9783034309455 (pb) £45.

With the recent spate of racist attacks in Northern Ireland, it seems clear that the architects of the local peace process have not yet fully realised their dream of a utopian, all-inclusive society. Against this backdrop, *Old Borders, New Technologies* engages with a range of experimental film and visual art that documents and interrogates Northern Ireland's troubled history, and speculates on the usefulness of these forms in post-conflict processes of healing. Drawing on notions of expanded cinema, Blair's study aims to explore and contextualise visual art practices which defy traditional notions of cinematic culture yet retain filmic elements in their form. She argues that these peripheral representations offer an alternative view to the highly mediated mainstream depiction of Northern Ireland that is still dominant in local and international public consciousness. She also suggests that a critique of these marginalised forms presents a potentially better understanding of the region's cultural history than one found in readings of the dominant mainstream representations of the conflict and its legacy. Blair identifies the fact that traditional studies of Northern Ireland's film-making have focused on the dramatic narrative and, in her attempt to locate experimental practices within a broader category of screen cultures, she calls for an expansion of thinking on the creation of visual arts in a post-conflict zone. The study problematises the notion of film in the twenty-first century with ever-expanding technological possibilities and a burgeoning range of diverse spectatorship positions.

The book is wide in its scope and theoretical engagements, touching on history, politics, gender, philosophy, national identity, media debates and anthropological concerns. In considering the theme of imprisonment, the study documents the extraordinary work of the Prisons Memory Archive and the Educational Shakespeare Company in recording prisoners' experiences and prison locations and in mobilising film as a vehicle for storytelling, both by directly documenting the complexity of incarceration in a charged political environment and by engaging with filmic representation as a cathartic dramatic form. Surveillance activities and technologies are illustrated by an examination of the work of artists Willie Doherty, Locky Morris and Allan Hughes which provides a commentary on the merging of gallery display and more traditional screen spaces, testifying to the fact that we live in a media saturated society in which we must search amid the plethora of

visual products for depictions that approximate to truthful representations. The startling performance art of Alastair MacLennan, André
Stitt, Sandra Johnston and Alanna O'Kelly is used to conceptualise
traumatic recall and the highly politicised notions of collective memory, while the experimental films of Duncan Campbell and the paintings of Robert Ballagh are engaged in order to illuminate processes of
myth-making. Much of the work explored raises challenging questions
about traditional spectatorship and the role of the viewer both in
creating meaning and, in a post-conflict location, enacting change.

Alongside a lively discussion of the local visual arts community, the
book navigates through a history of various international art practices
in an informative and useful way. Richly illustrated with stills, it
also provides a detailed textual reconstruction of various exhibitions,
installations and instances of staged performance art – typically forms
that resist traditional archiving. The notion of the ethics of the
appropriation of archival material also forms part of the discussion,
alongside an exploration of the positioning of the human body in
visual art forms. As such, the book will be of interest to students of
film, art and the history of both, as well as to scholars, film-makers,
visual artists and community activists in Northern Ireland and other
post-conflict zones.

Blair's claim that, through exploring these artistic practices and
utilising them in educational contexts, healing may occur, is perhaps
overly idealistic. But her point that experimental visual art practices
reveal a screen culture that abounds in social value and transcends
the traditionally market-oriented film industry in Northern Ireland
is a powerful reminder of the significance of non-mainstream and
marginalised artistic practices in deeply interrogating social fabrics
and hegemonic structures. Baker and McLaughlin suggest in *The
Propaganda of Peace* (2010) that the 'extraordinary transformations
in Northern Irish society have been attended by the truncation of
political debate and the impoverishment of the cultural imagination',
clarifying that 'dissenting voices have been marginalized or maligned,
political activism viewed as disruptive of the social order and pacified
domesticity presented as the preferred model of citizenship' (13). The
artistic practices explored in *Old Borders, New Technologies* are certainly
marginal in their dissemination, radical in their content and an
essential part of the liminal discourses of Northern Irish culture. They
mount a challenge to the traditional, market-driven impetus to create
a globalised, financially successful film industry in Northern Ireland,
instead calling on local artists to produce work that interrogates the
past in both form and content in order to move towards a healthy

society in which political debate is rich and nuanced and real social change is possible. This book makes a valuable contribution to debates on the importance of a vibrant cultural imagination as a means of understanding both the legacies of conflict and also the legacies of its representation.

Ciara Chambers (University of Ulster)
DOI: 10.3366/jbctv.2014.0237